Dragons with Pets

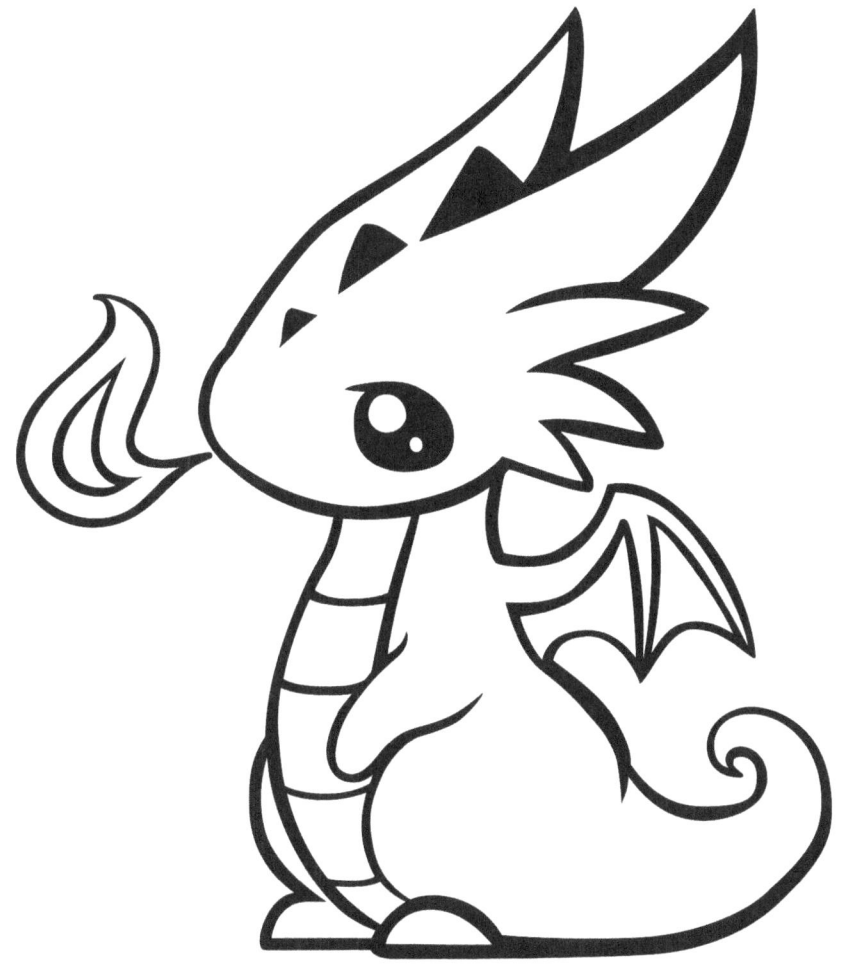

Coloring Book by
Dragons and Beasties

Copyright © 2017 by Dragons and Beasties
Illustrated by Becca Golins

All rights reserved. This book or any portion thereof may not be reproduced or used in any manner without the express written permission from Dragons and Beasties.

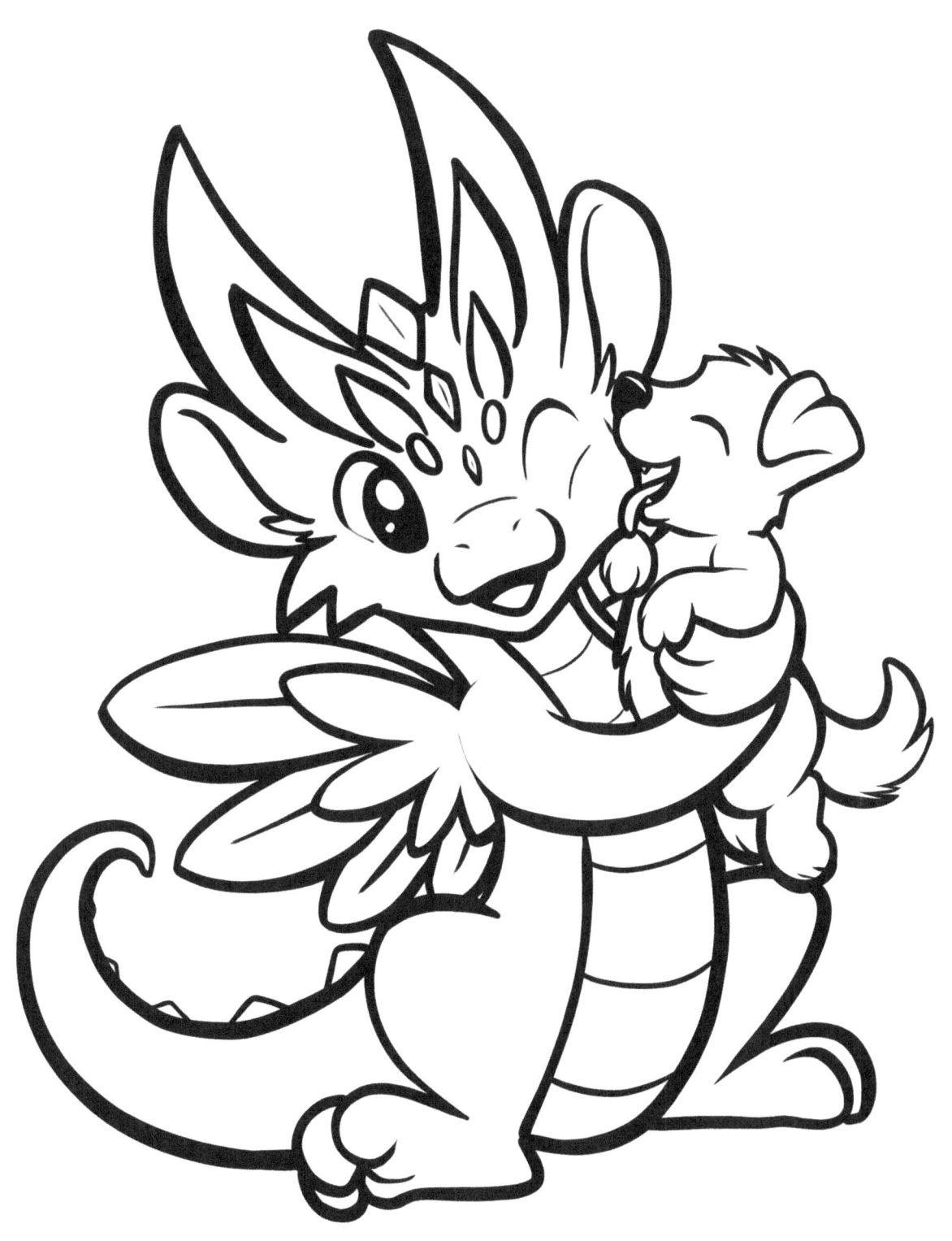

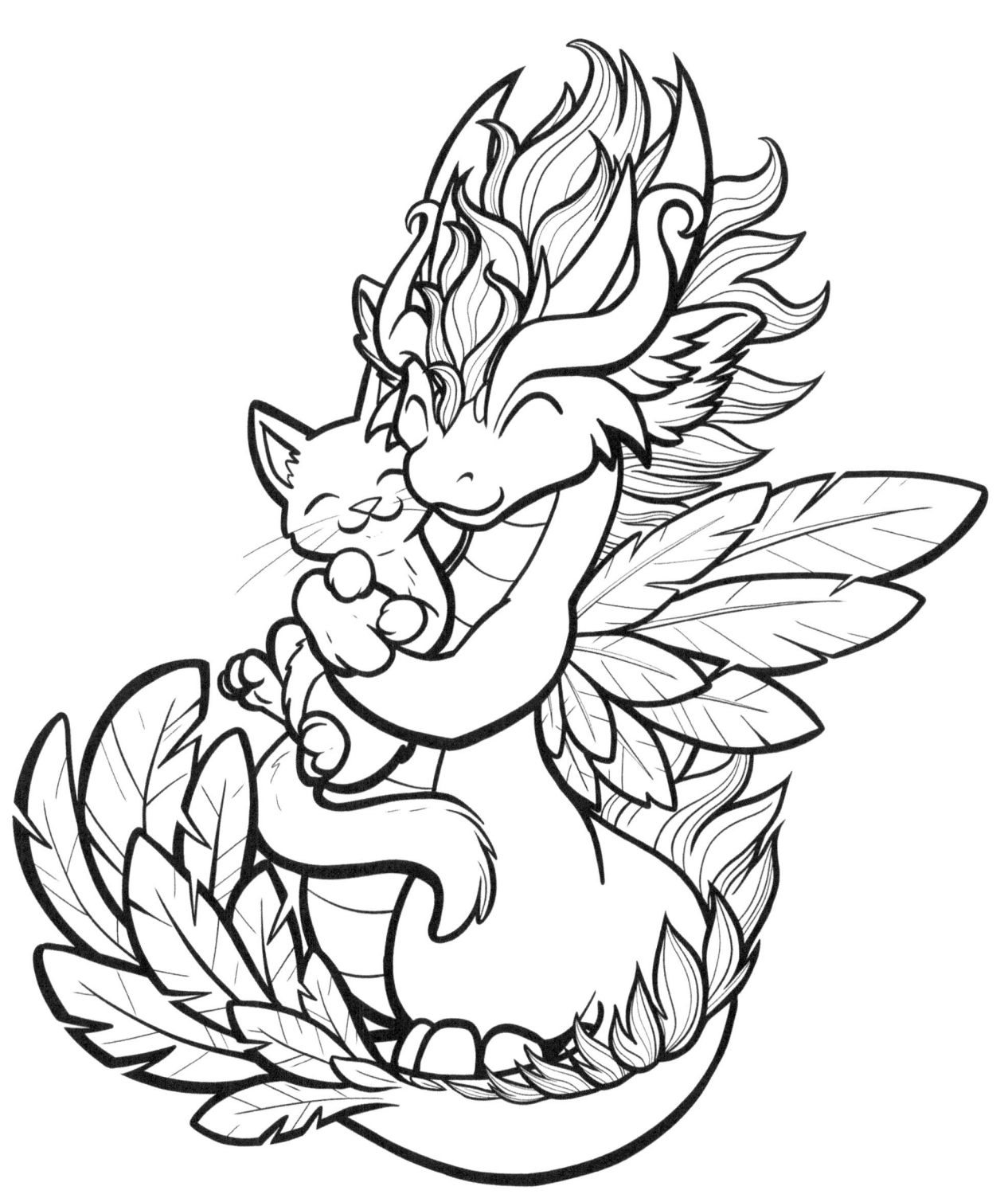

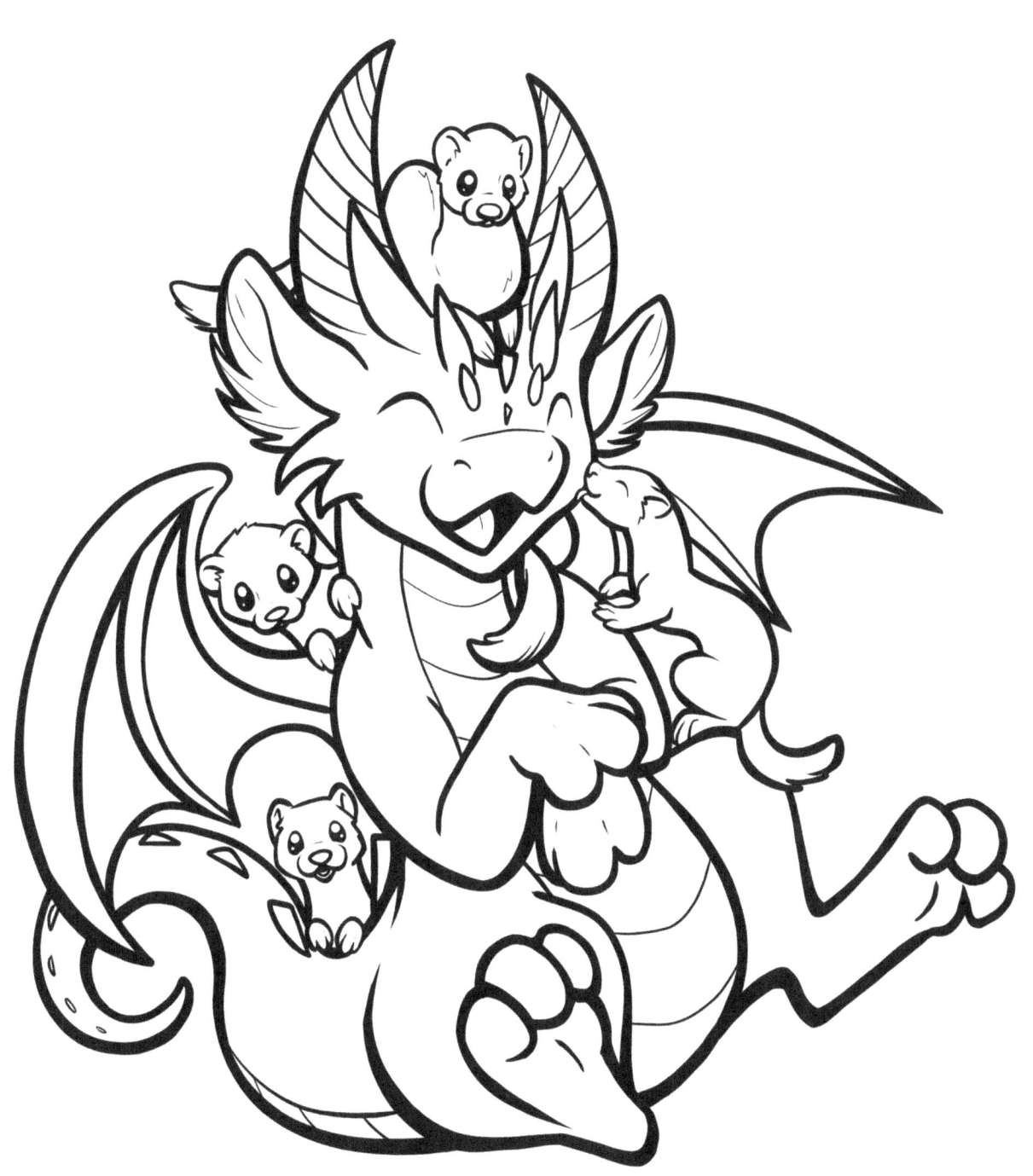

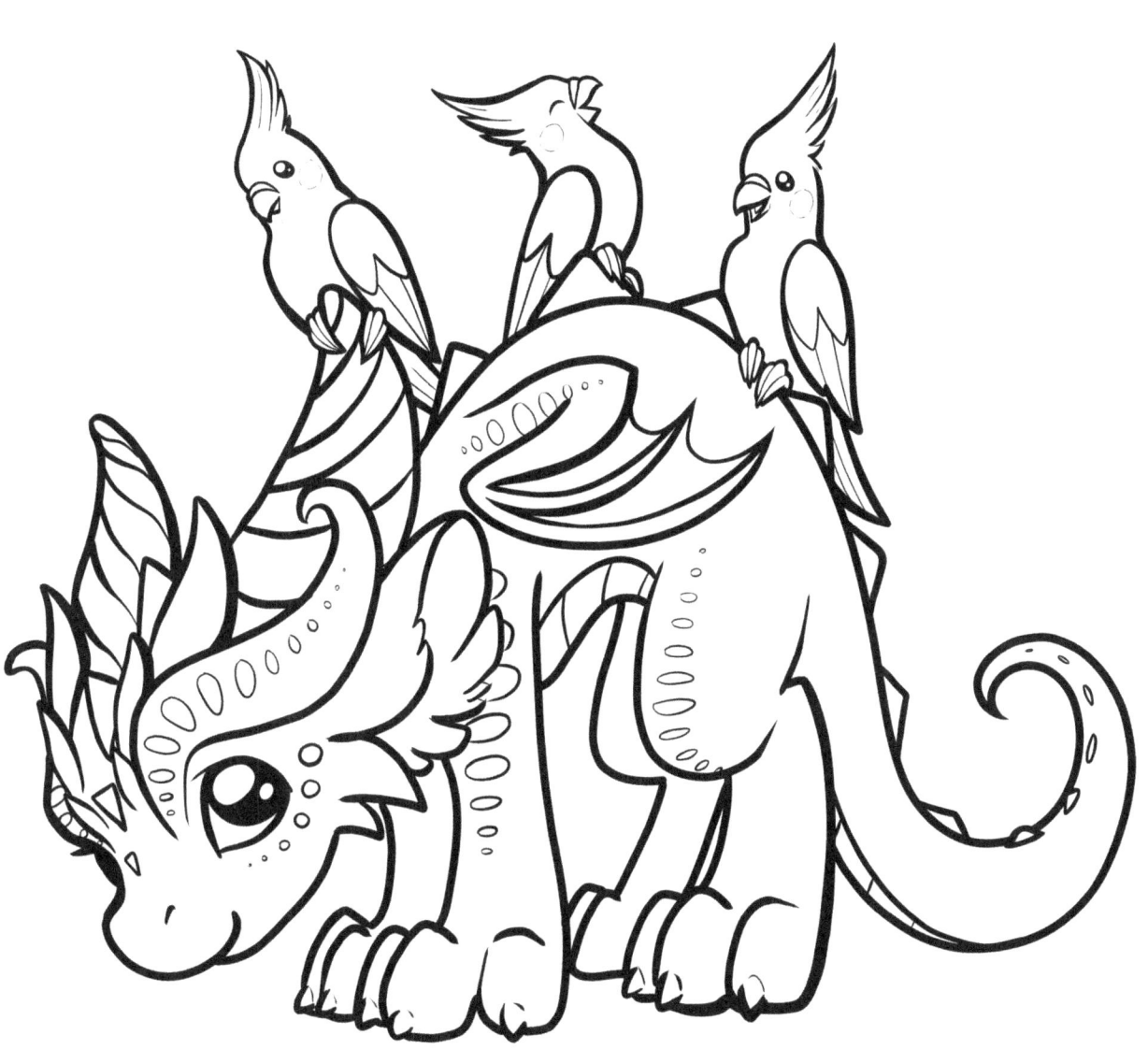

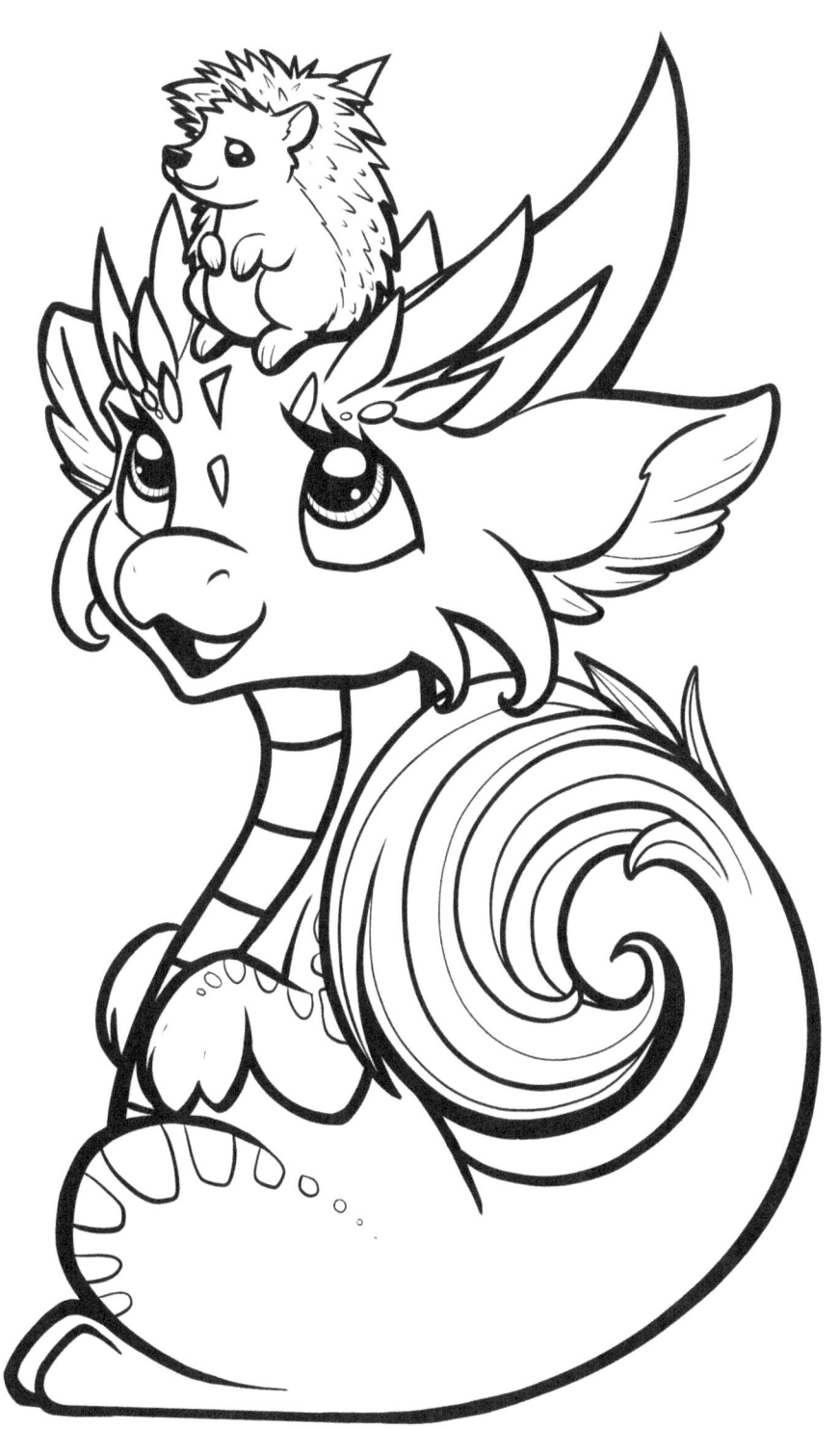

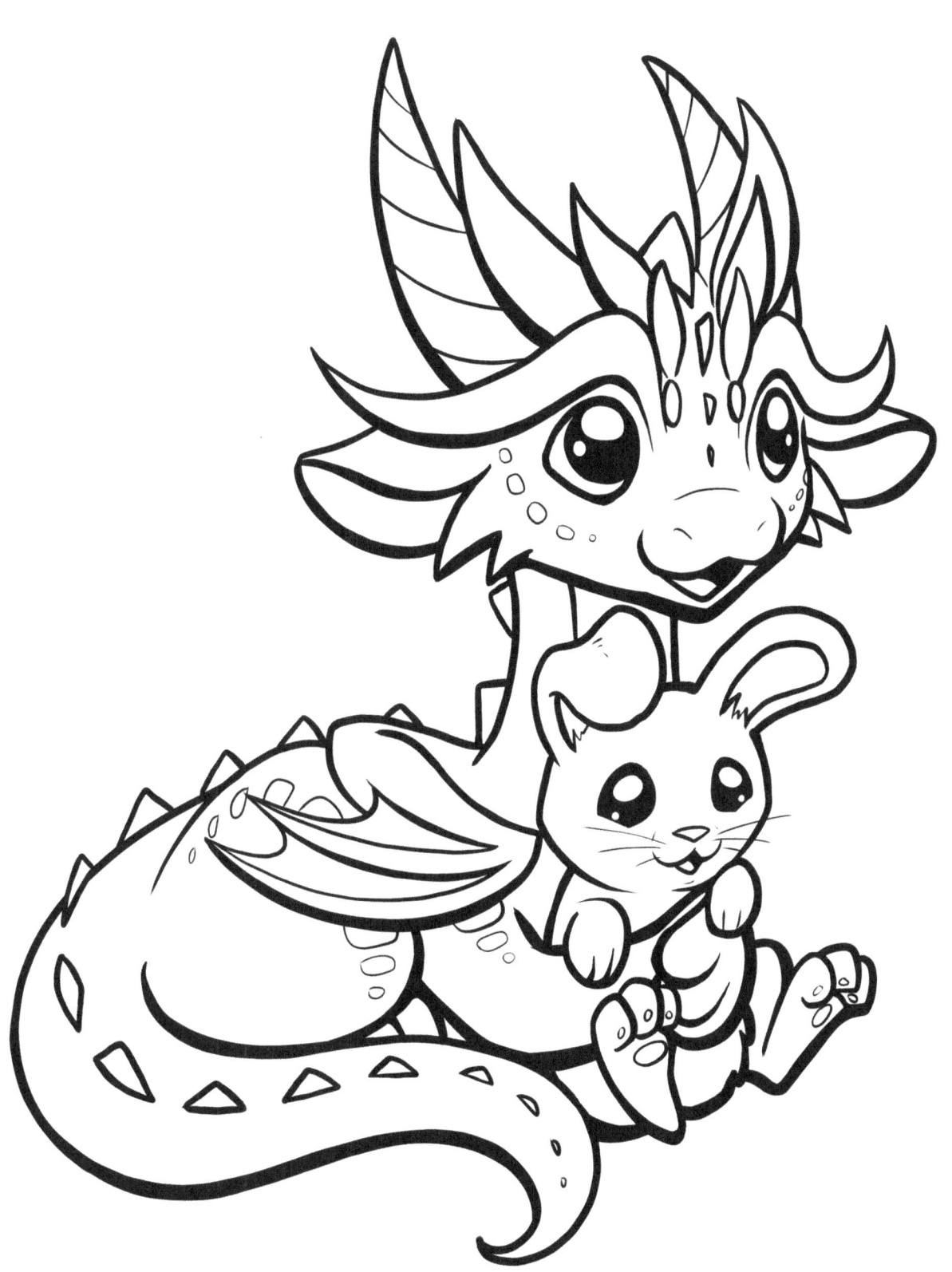

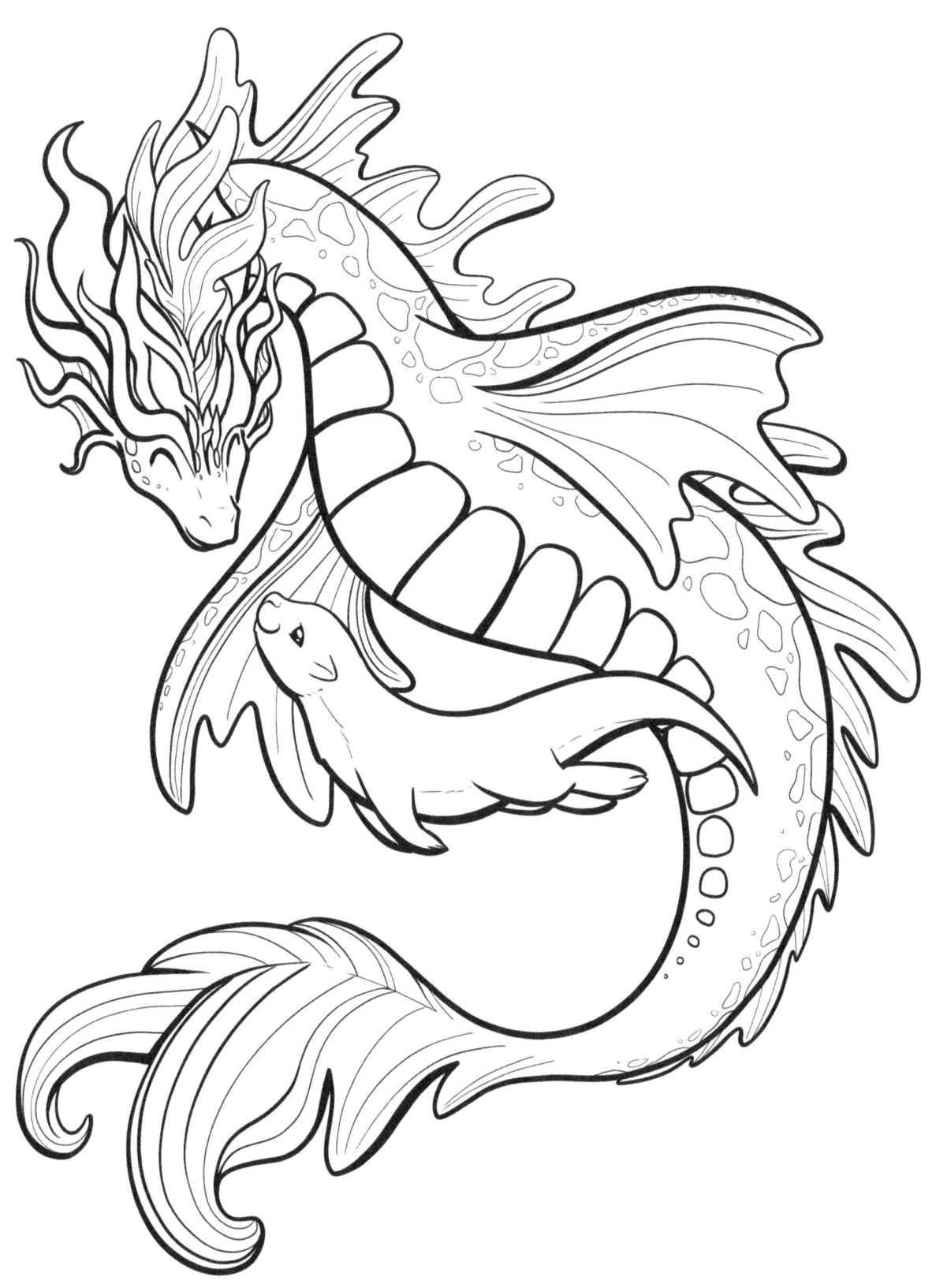

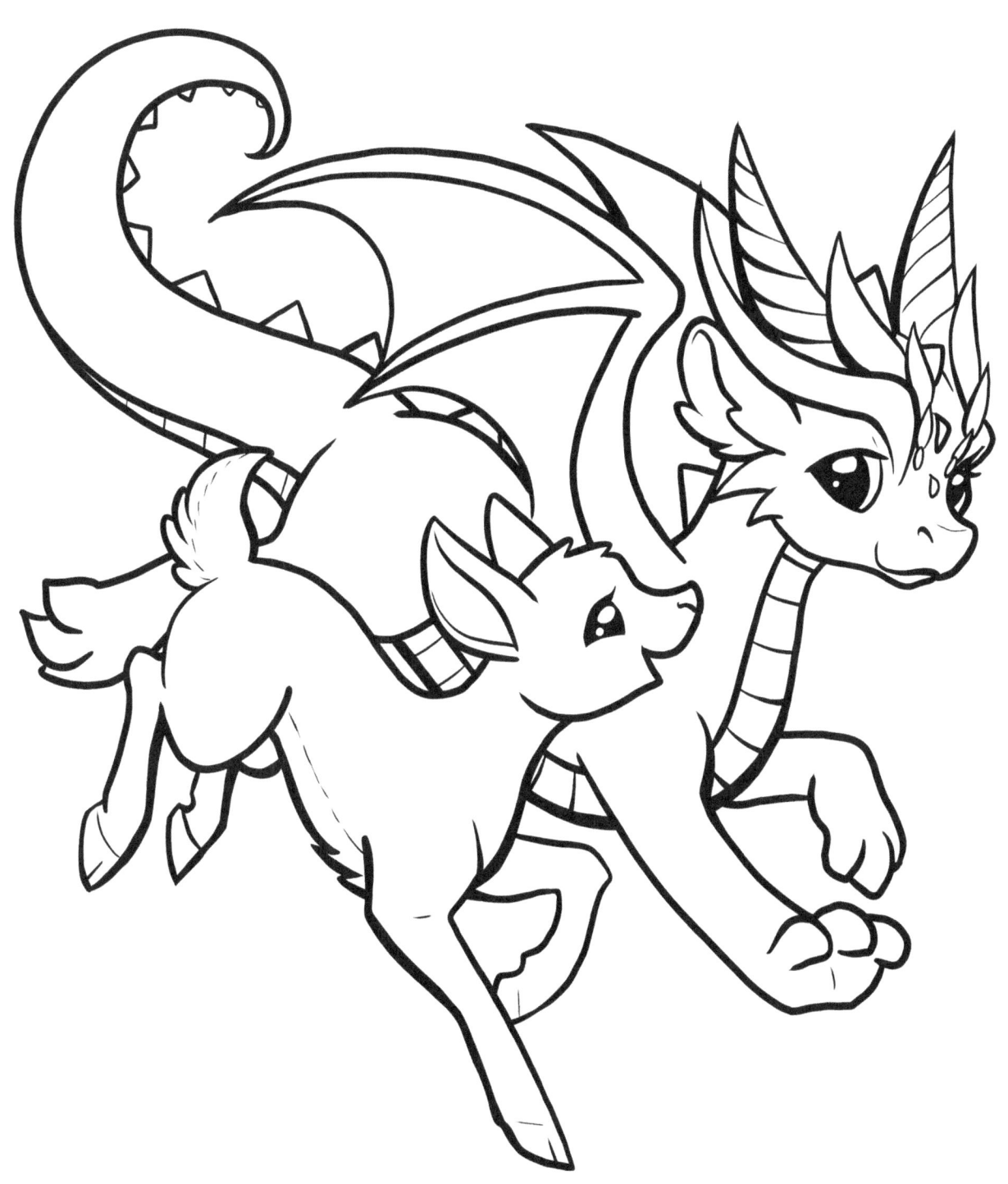

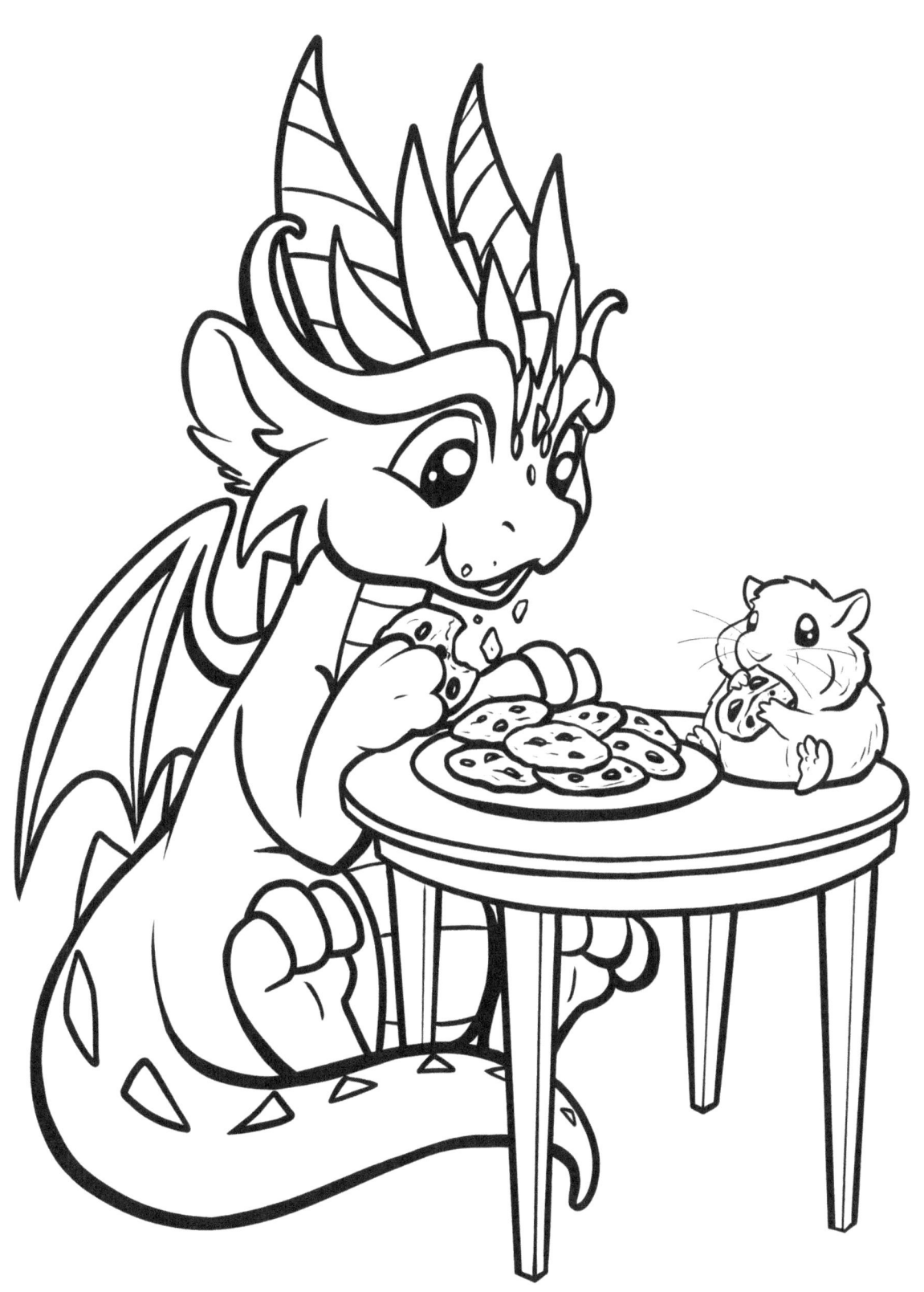

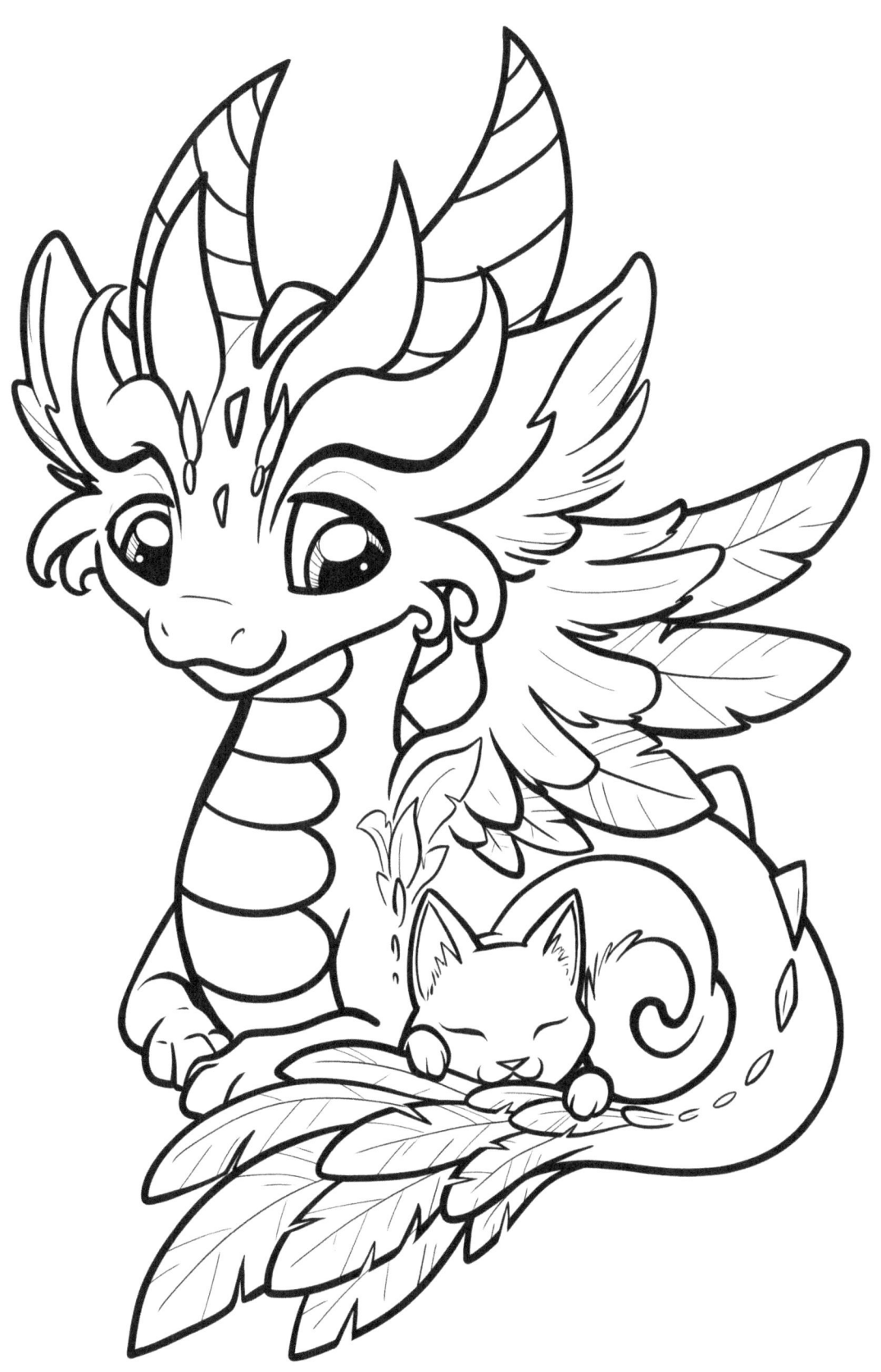

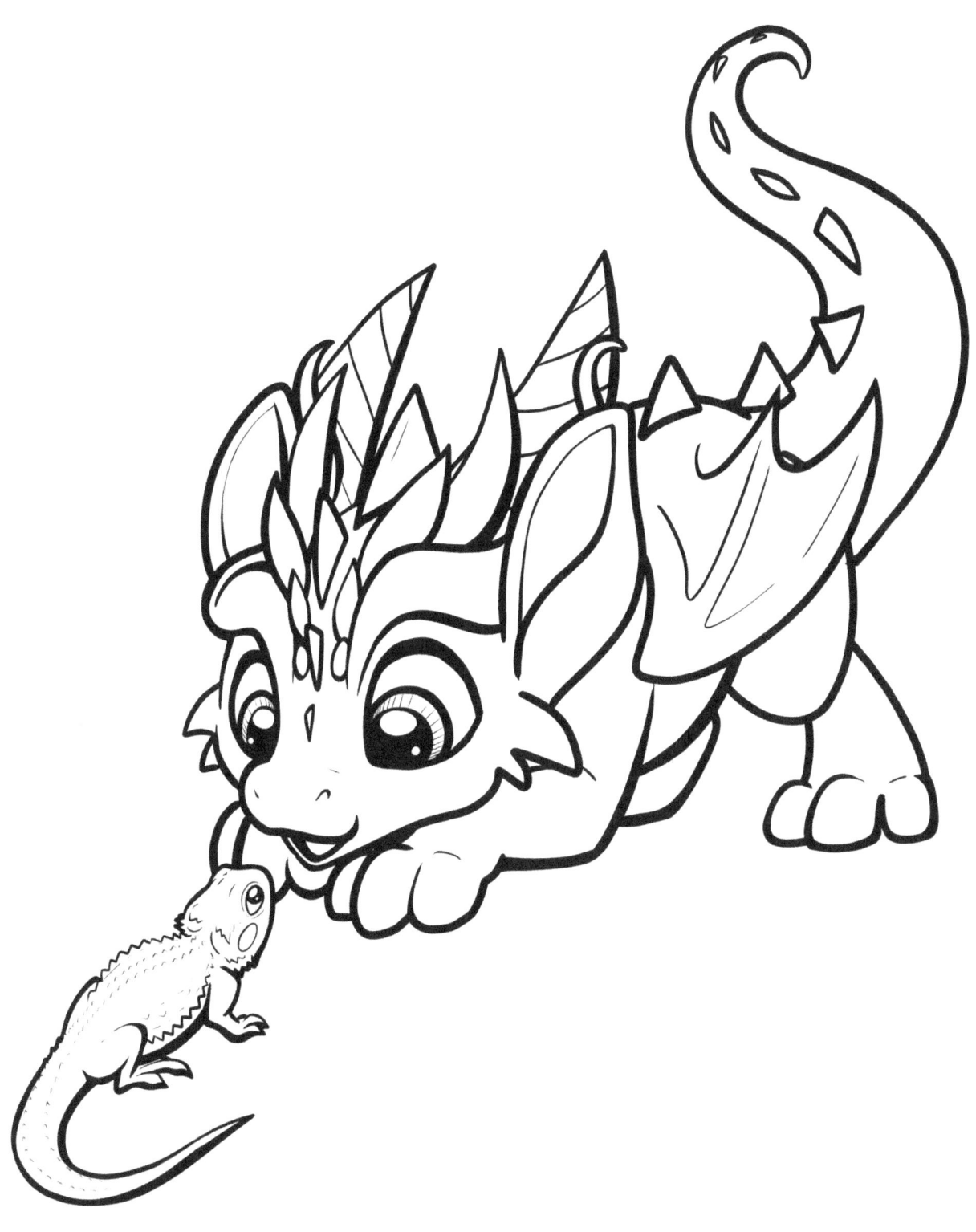

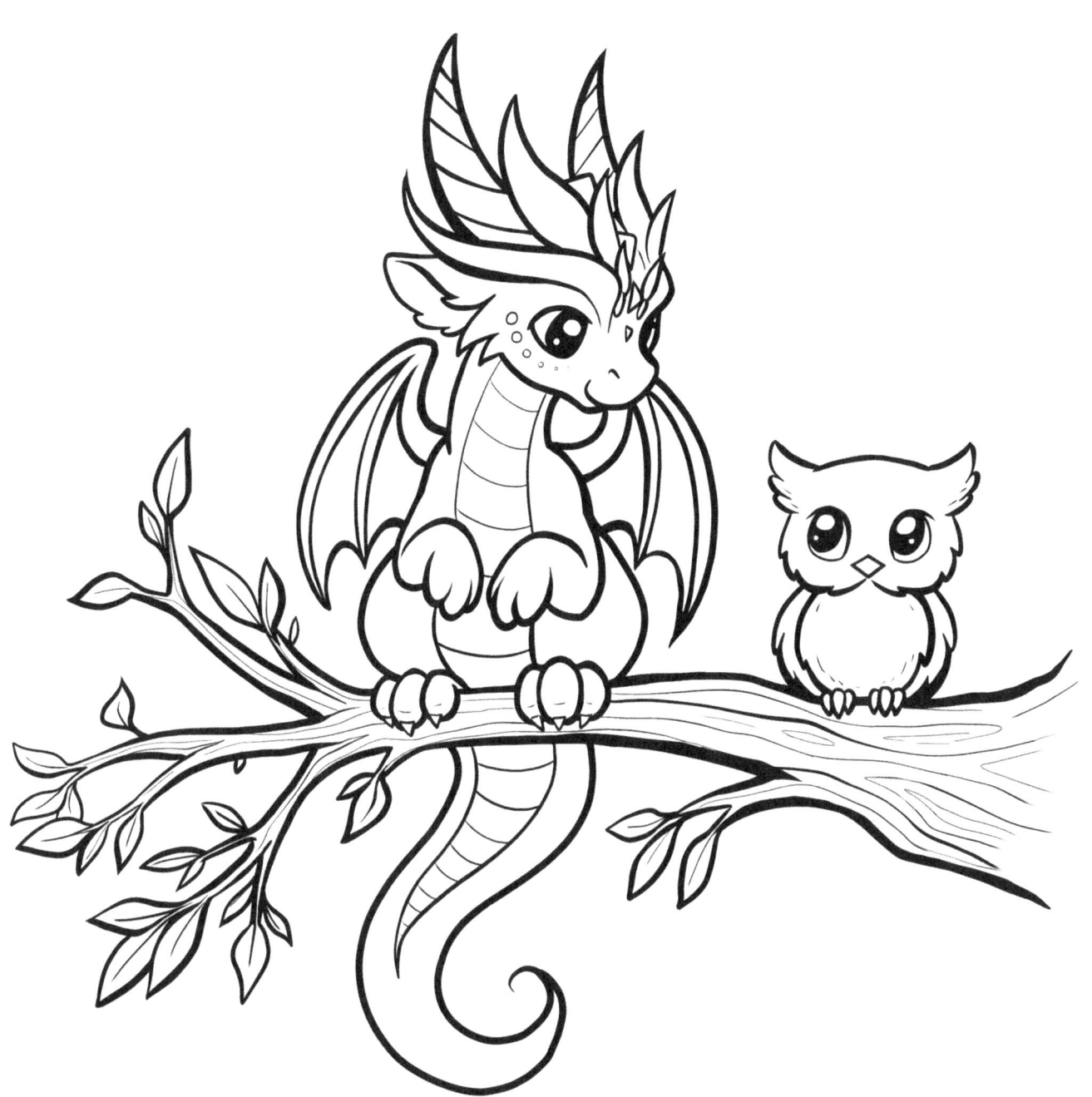

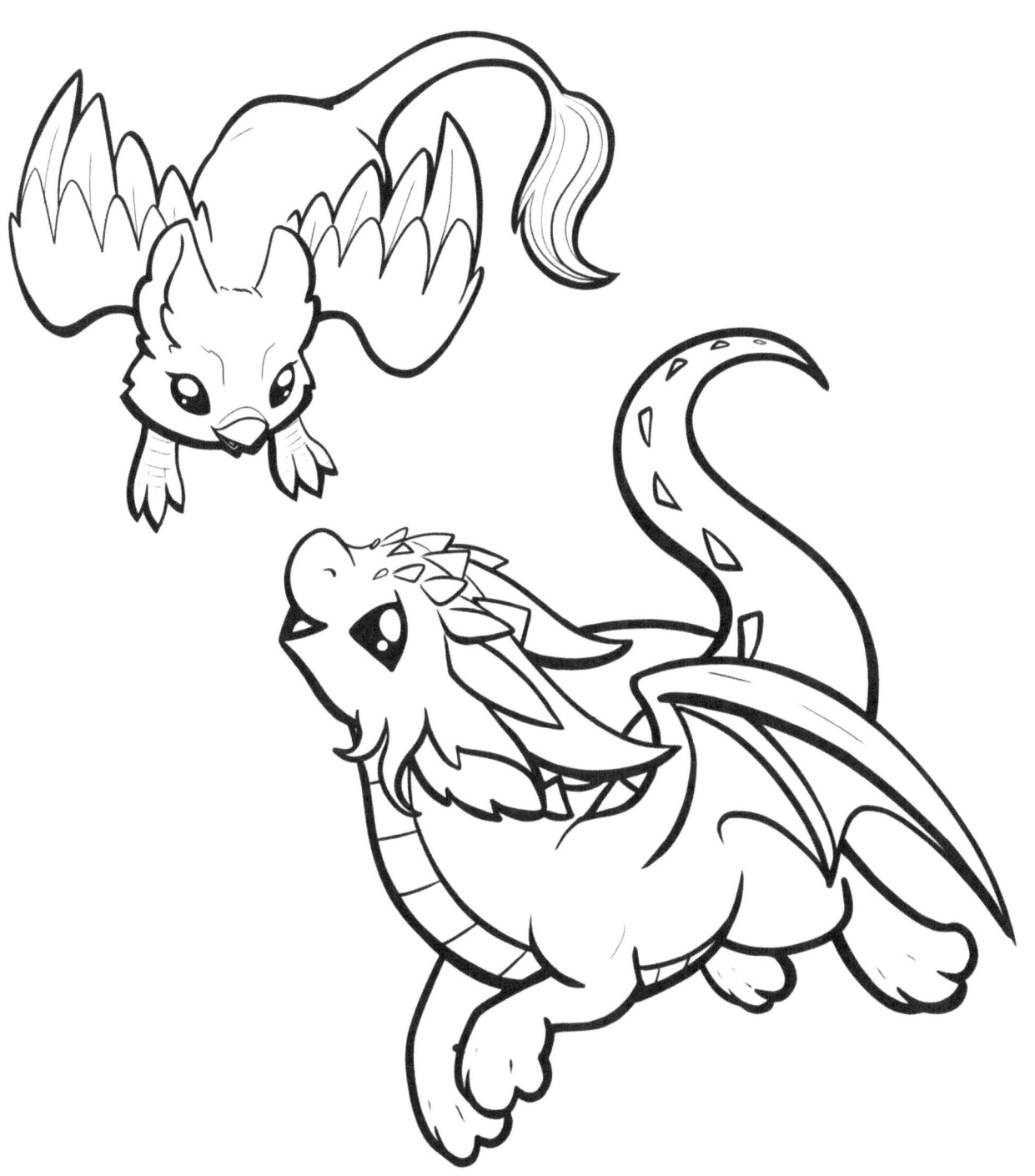

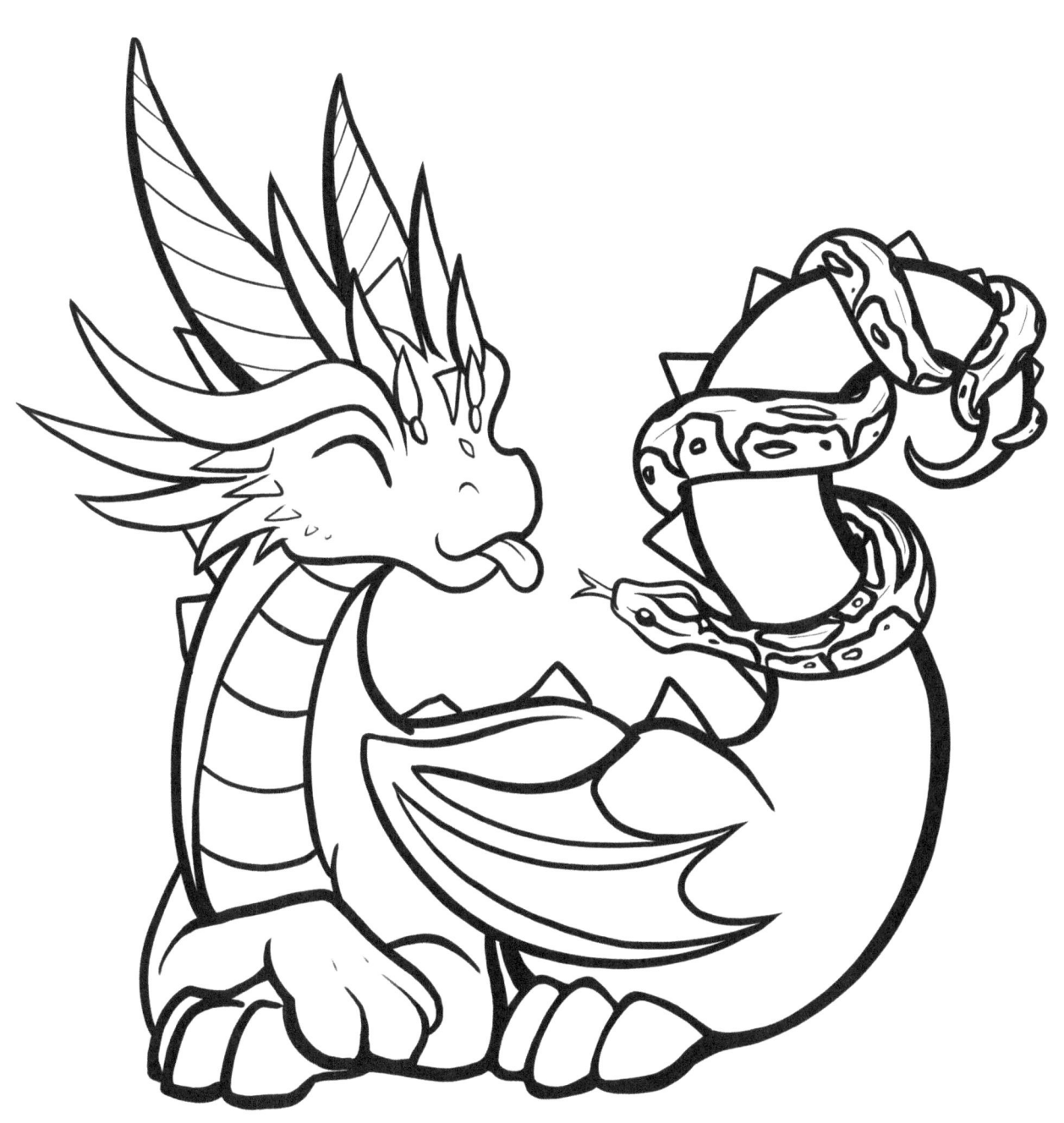

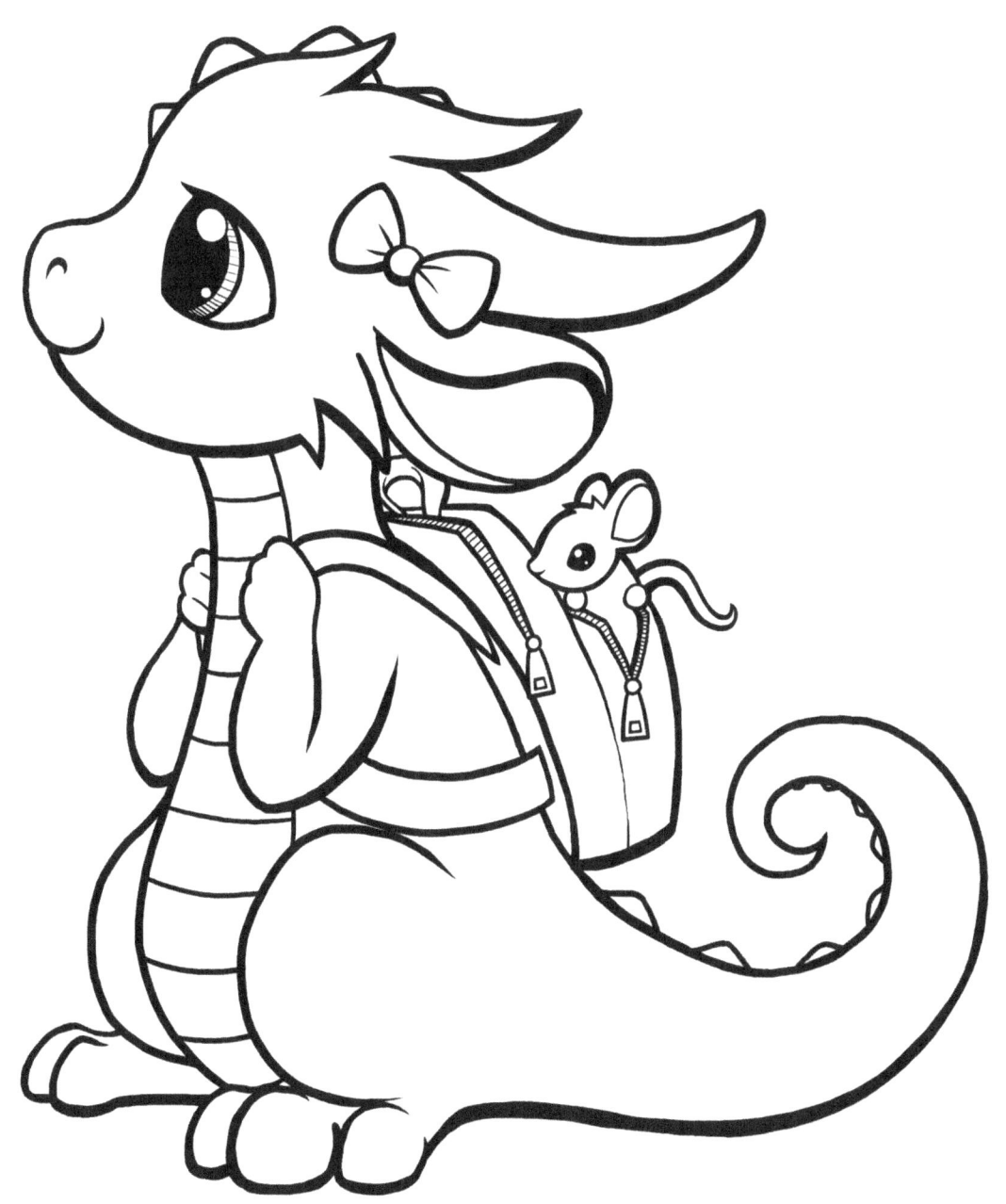

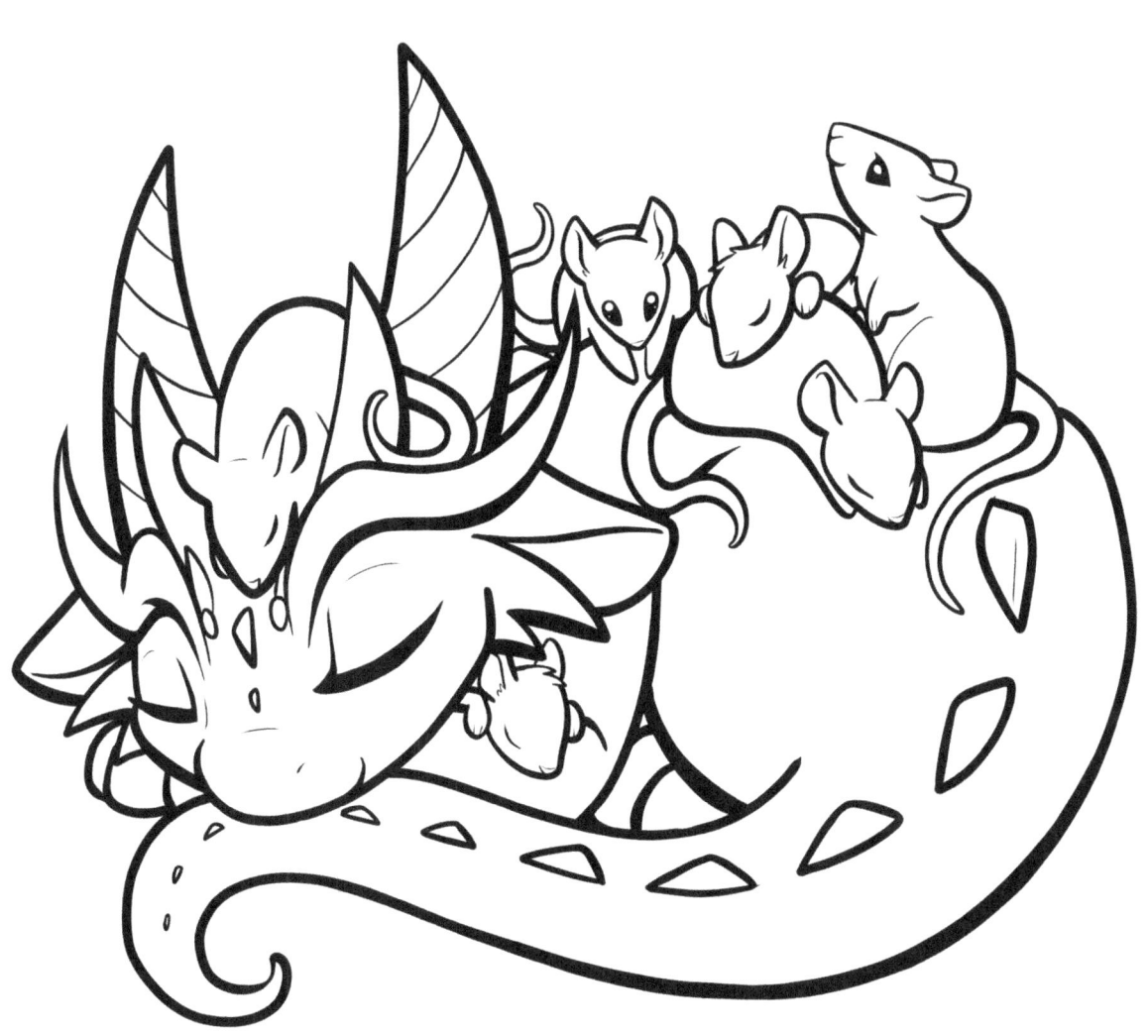

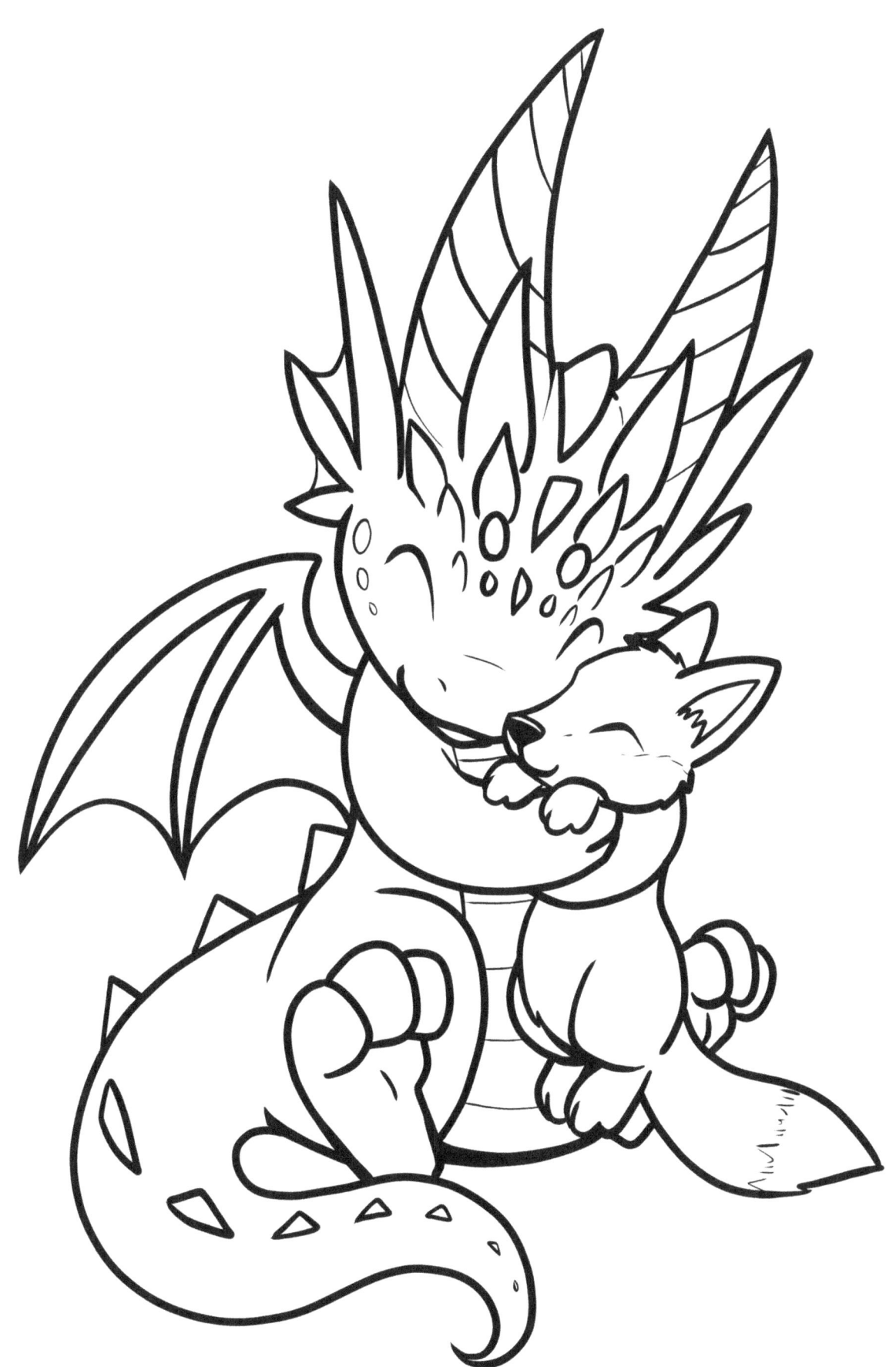

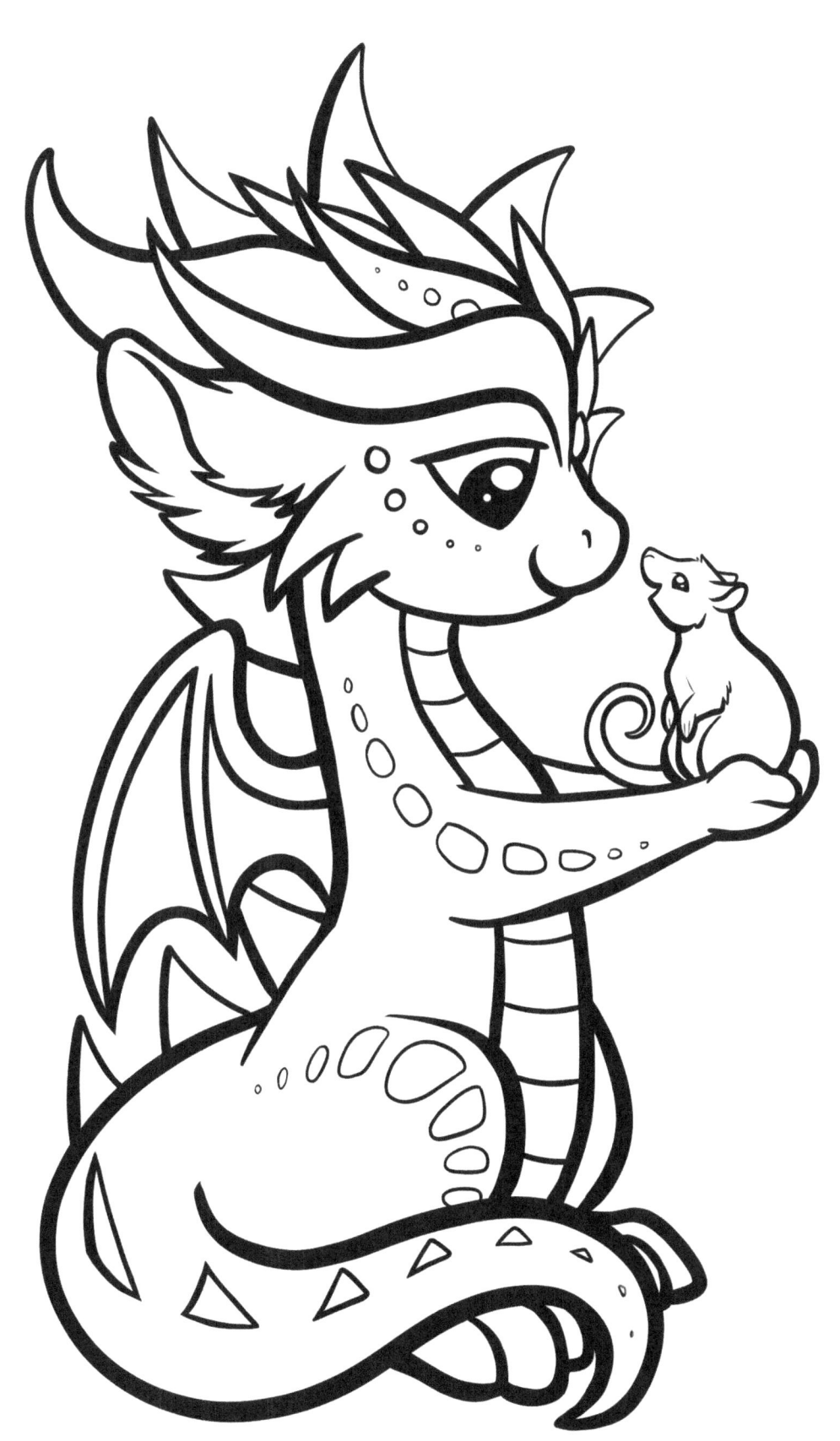

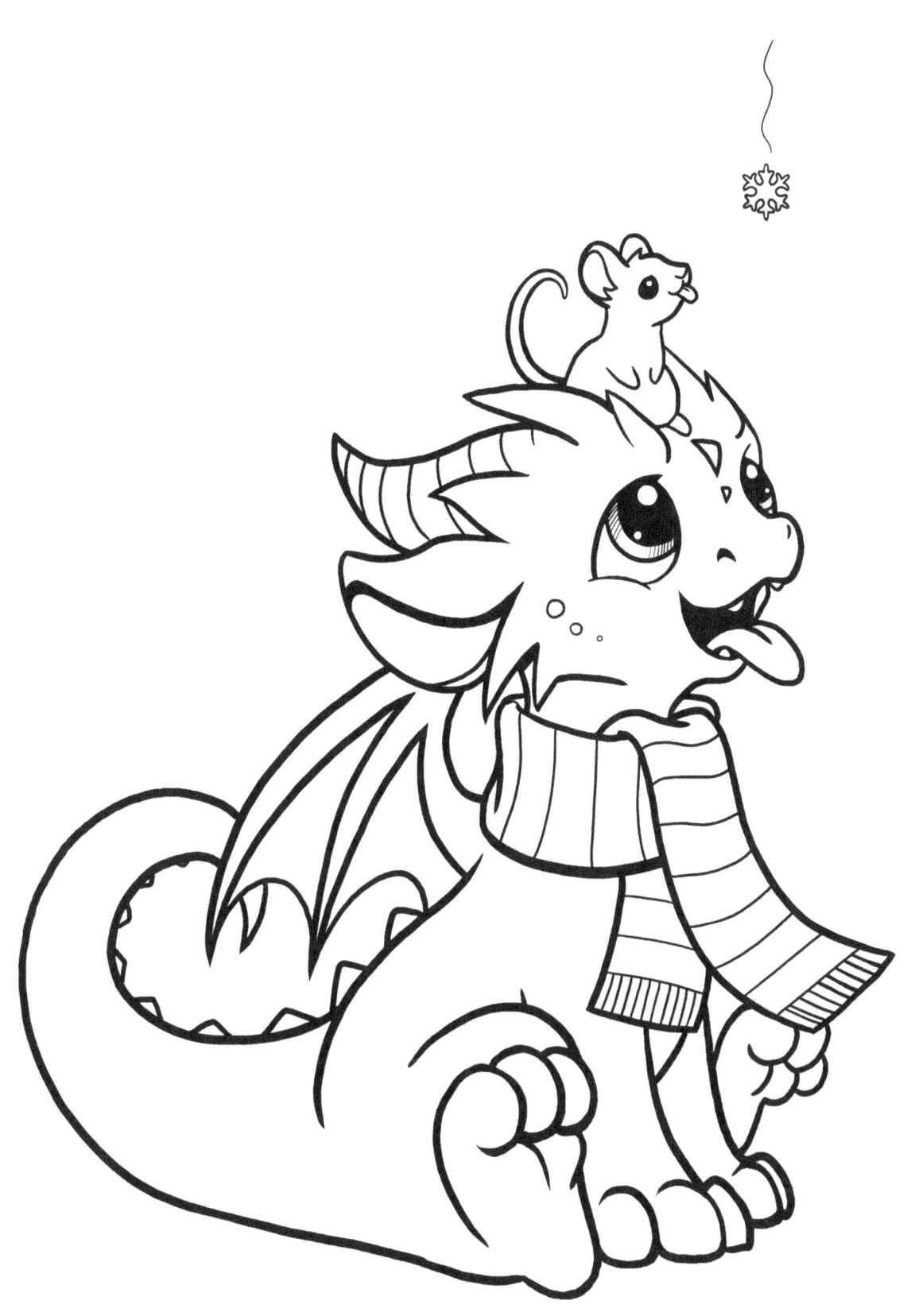

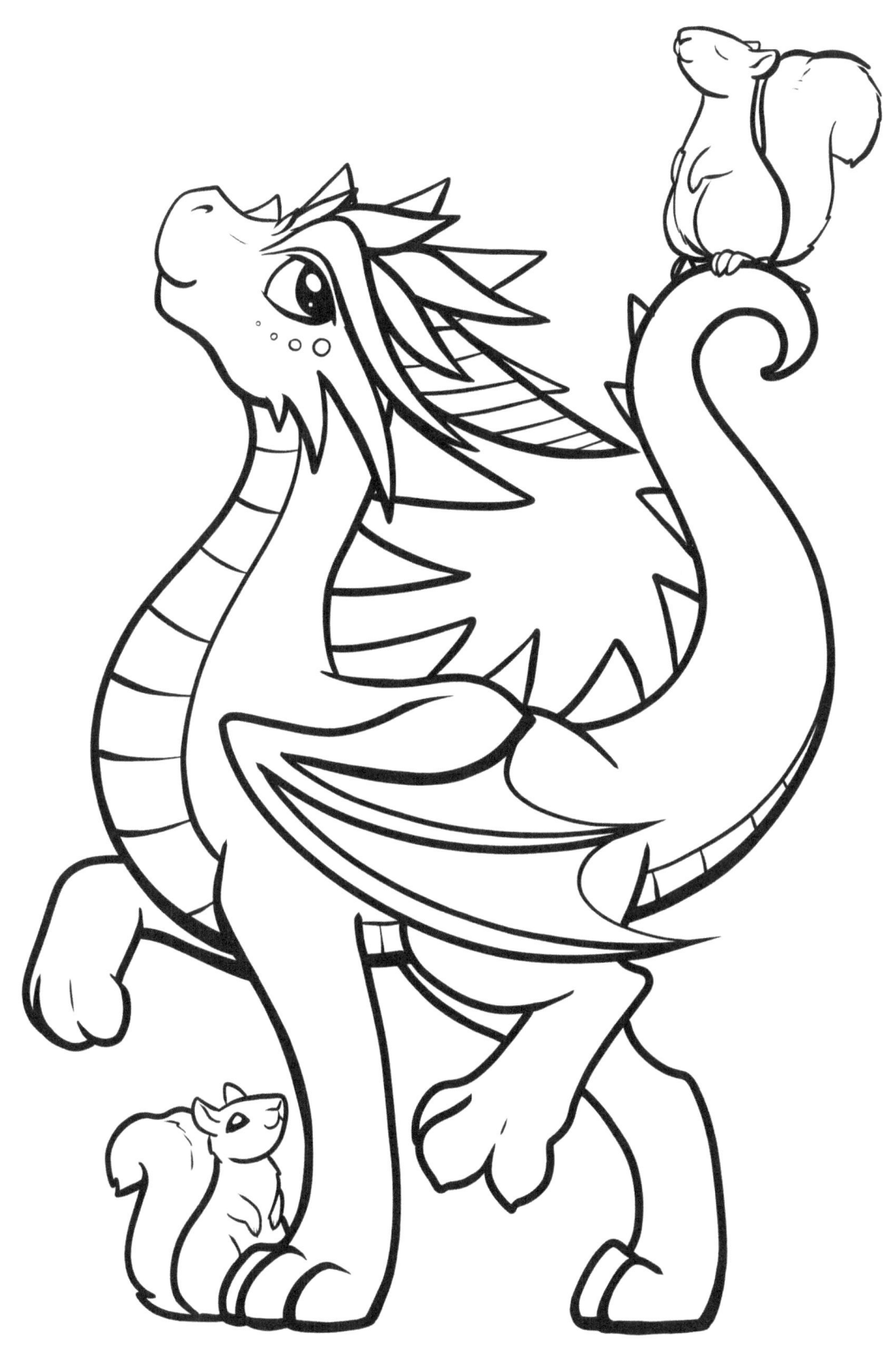

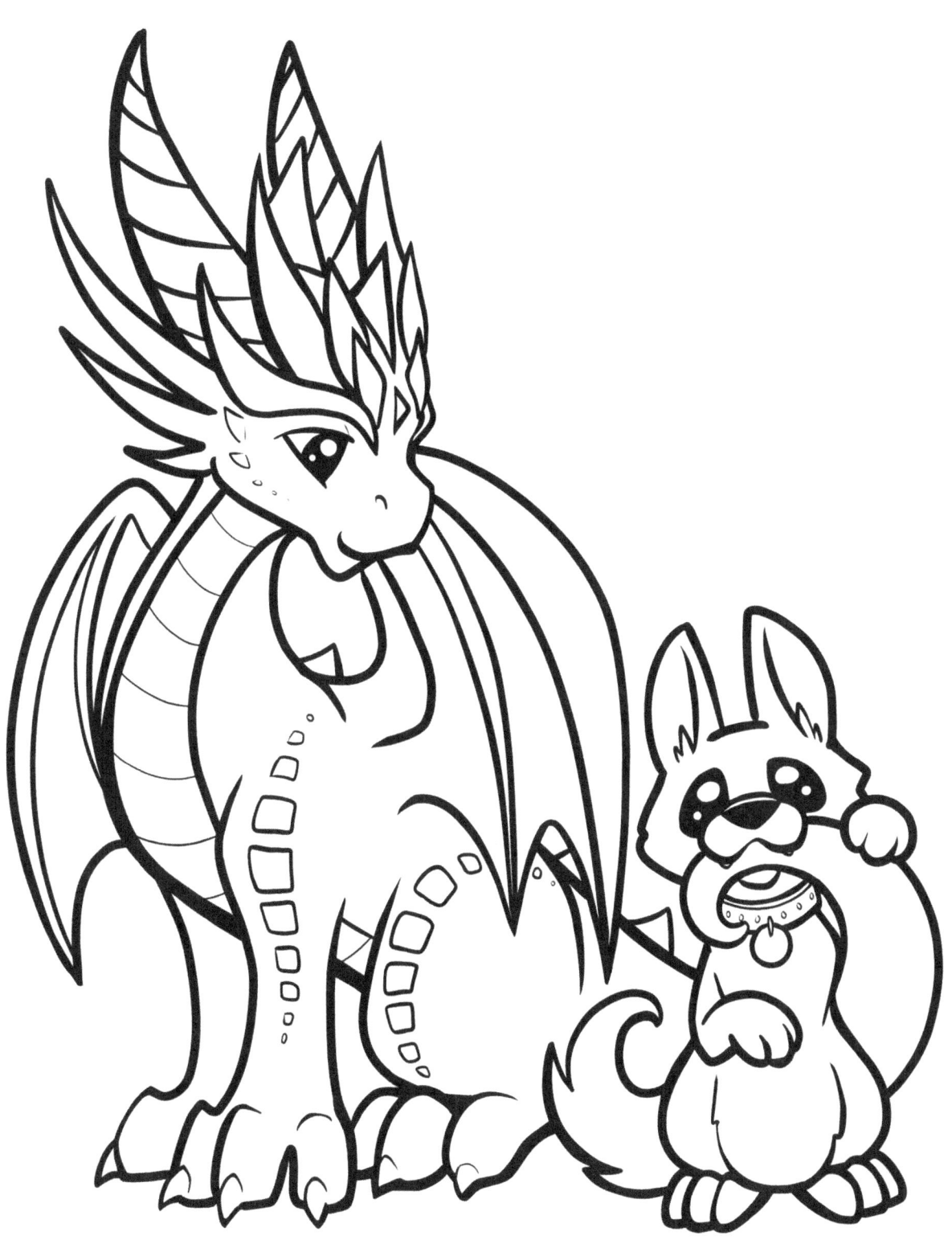

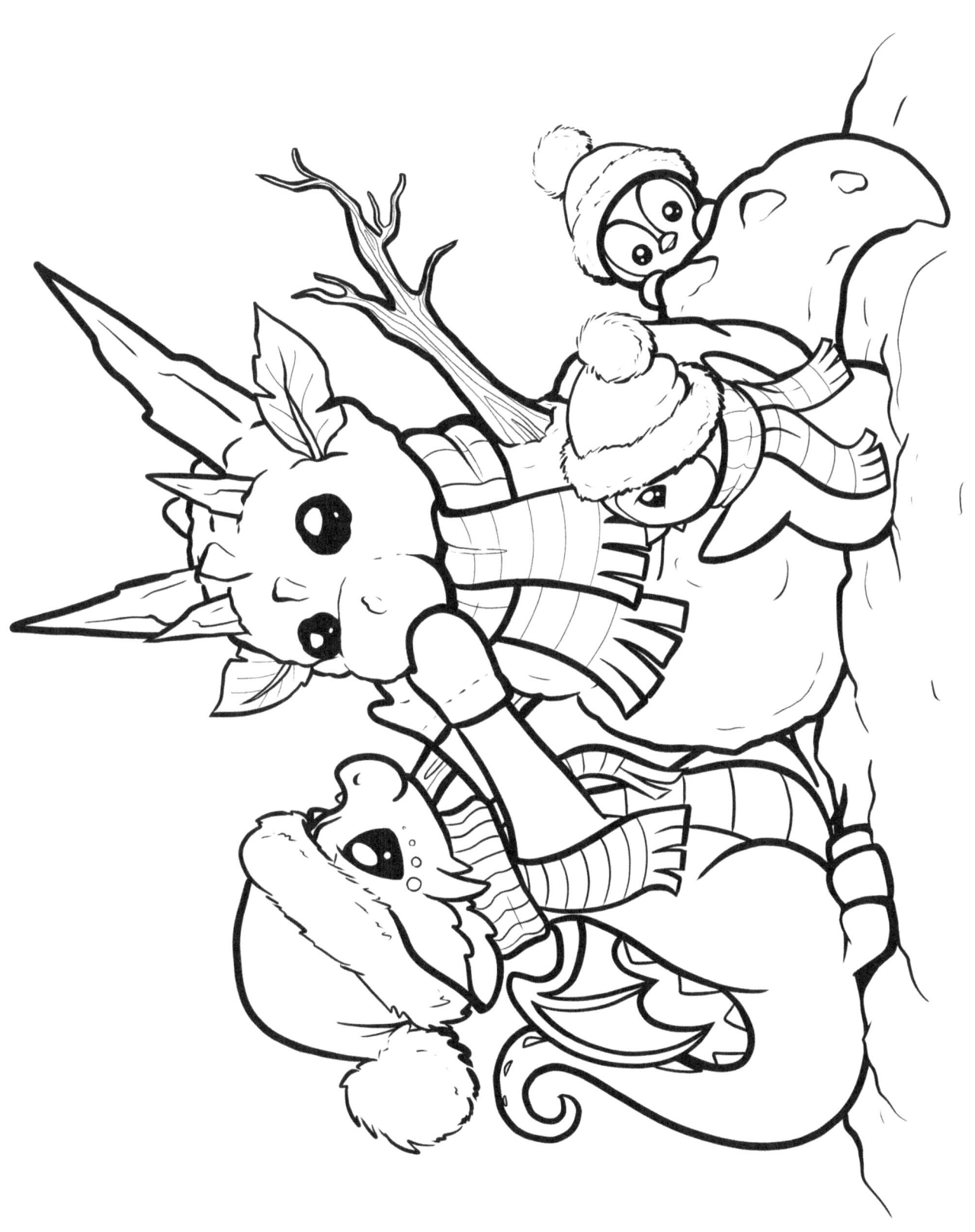

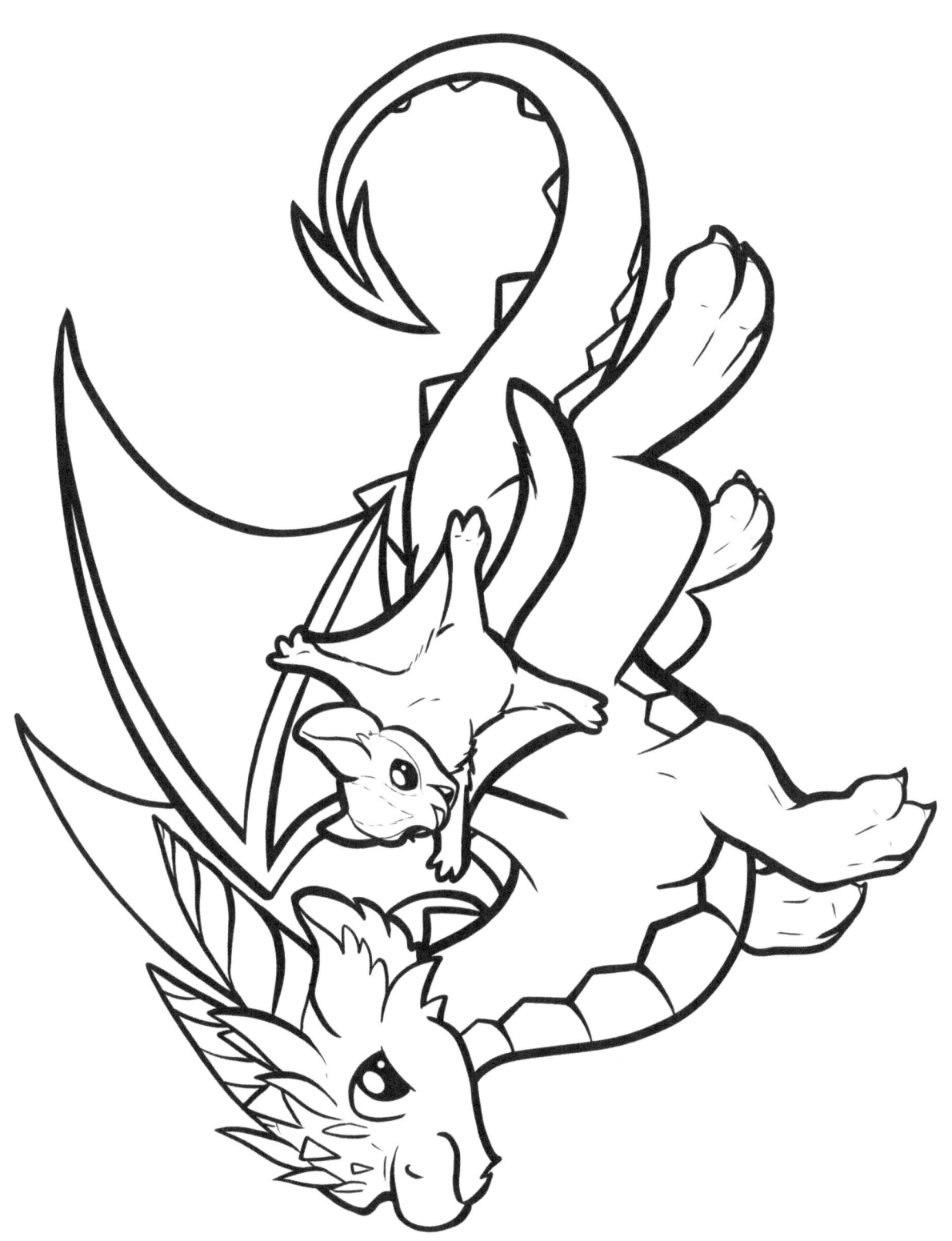

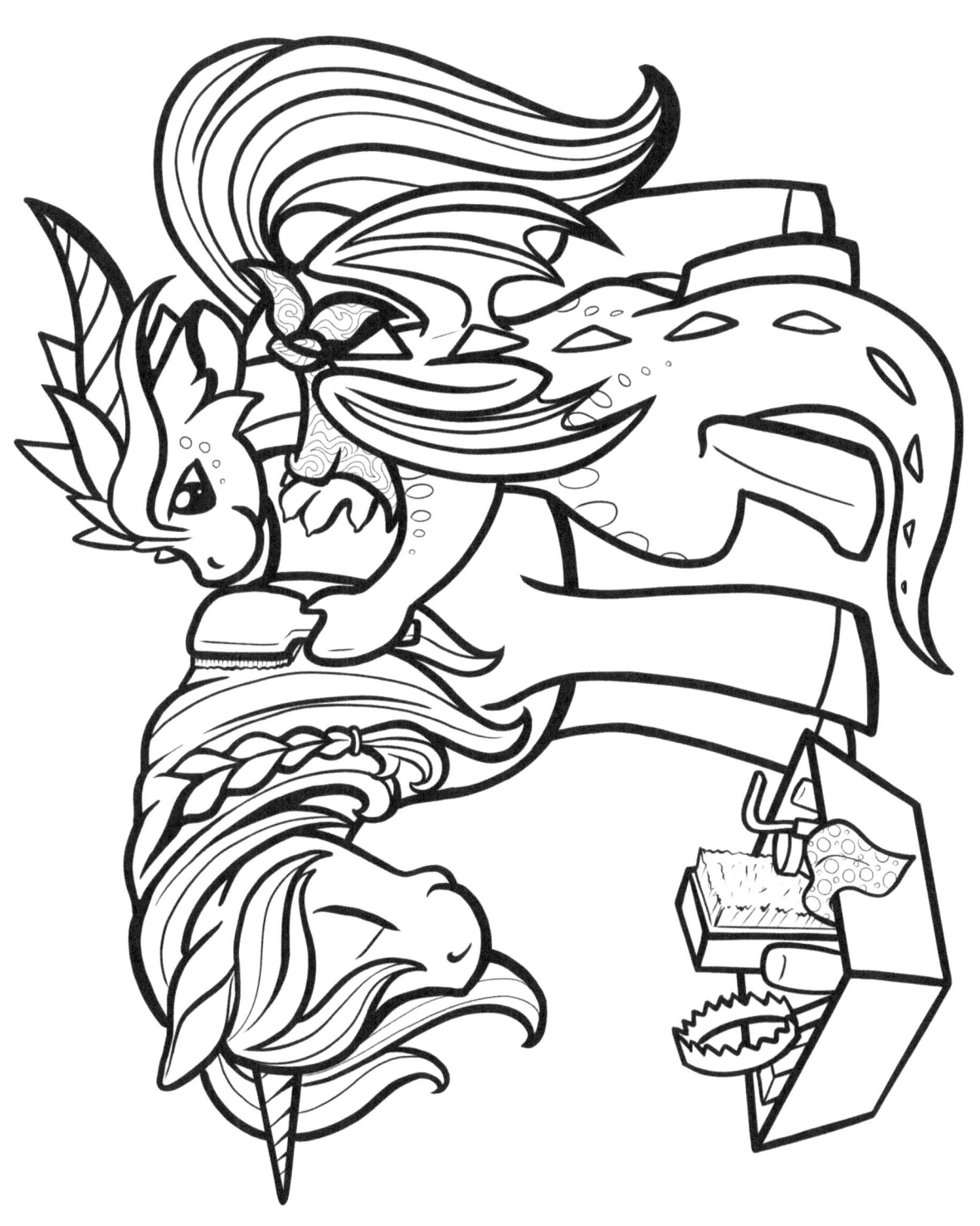

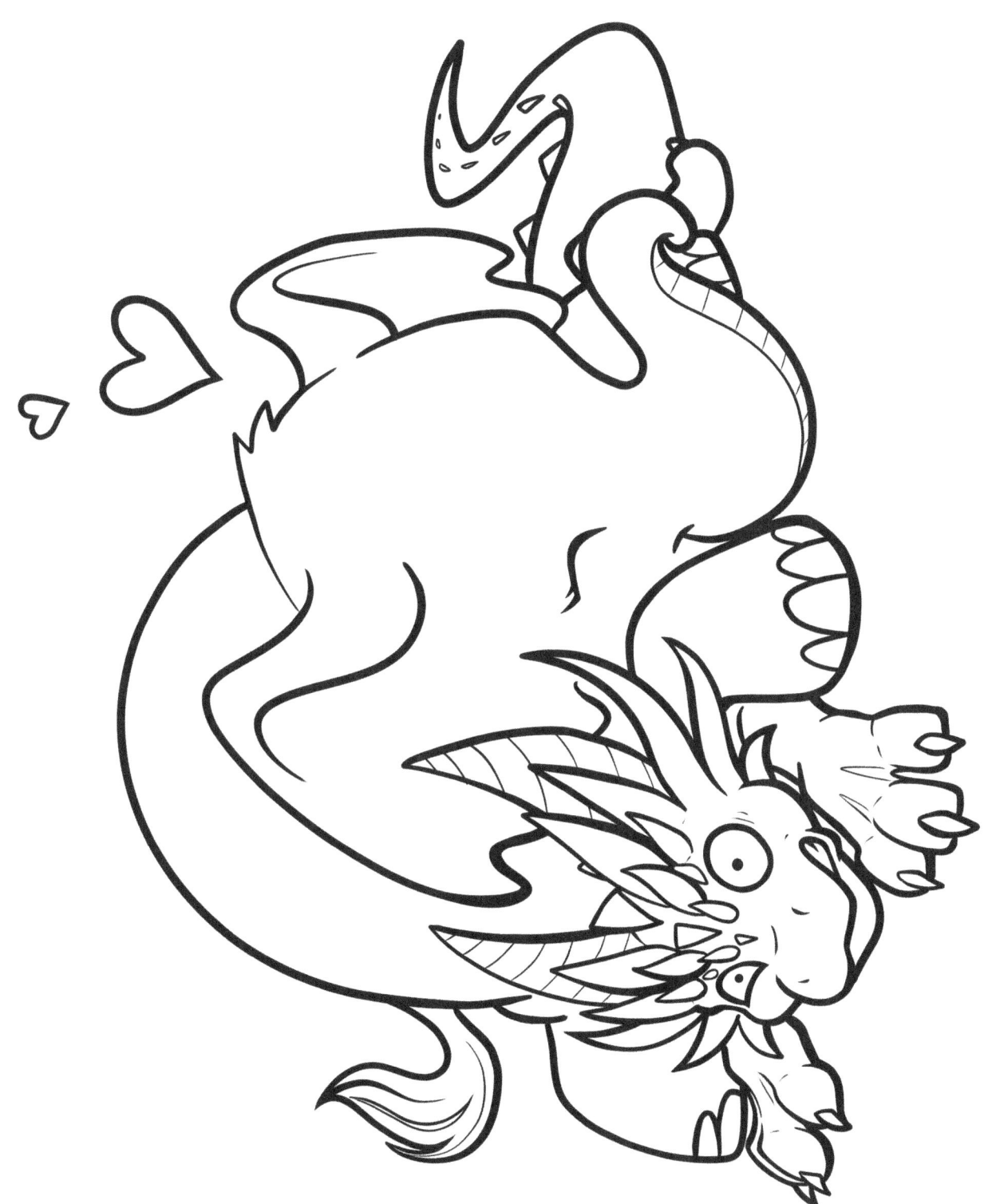

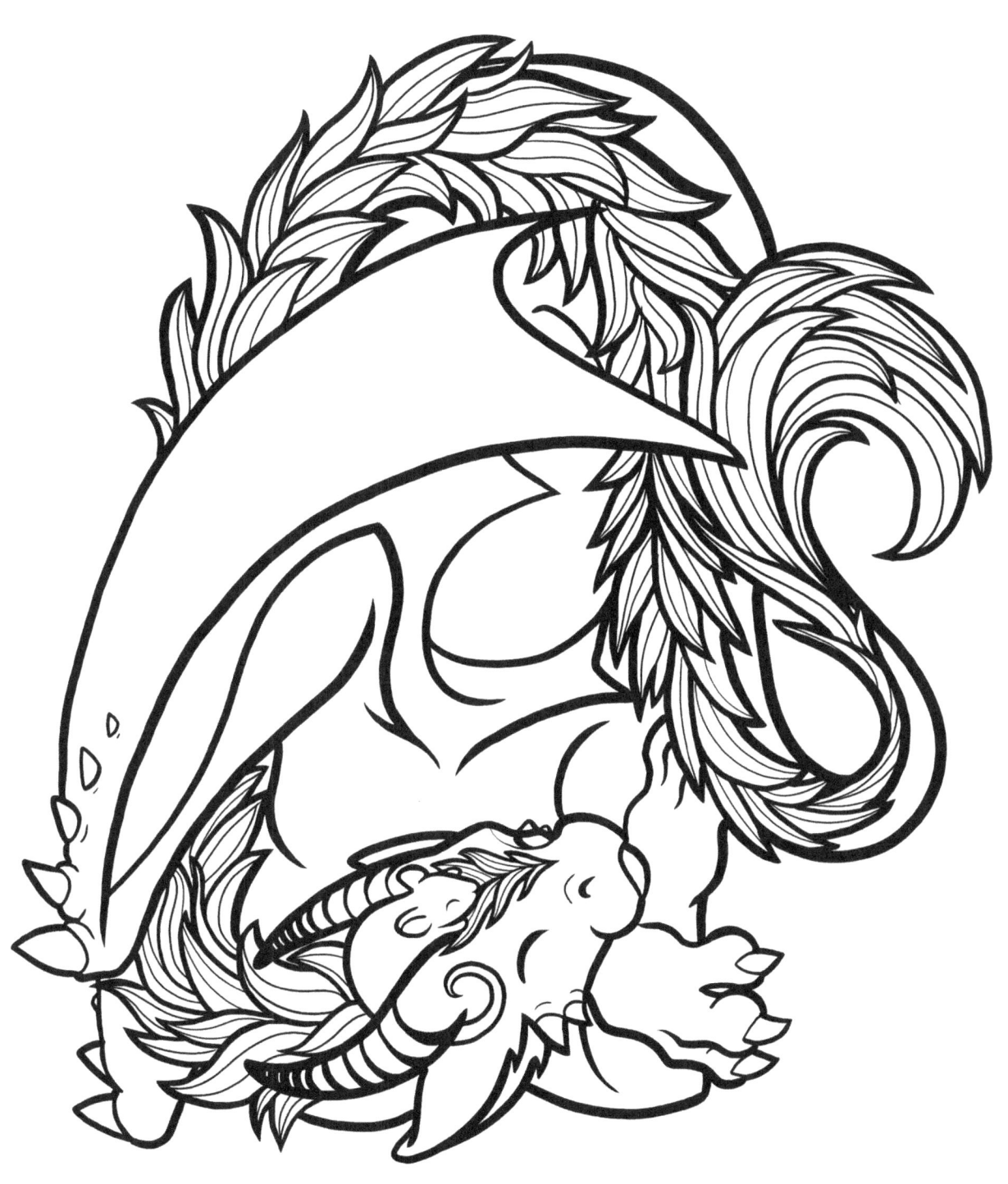

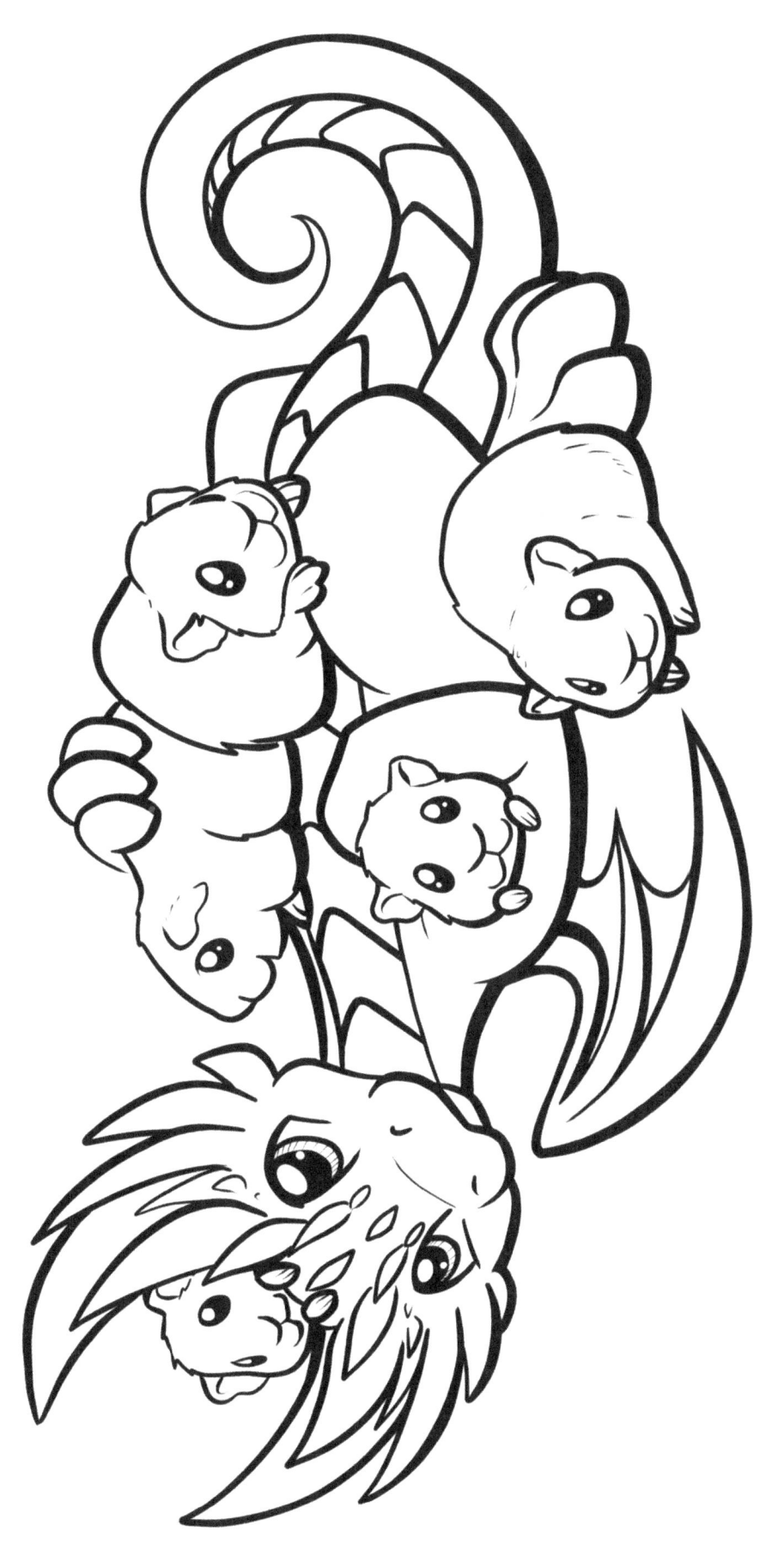

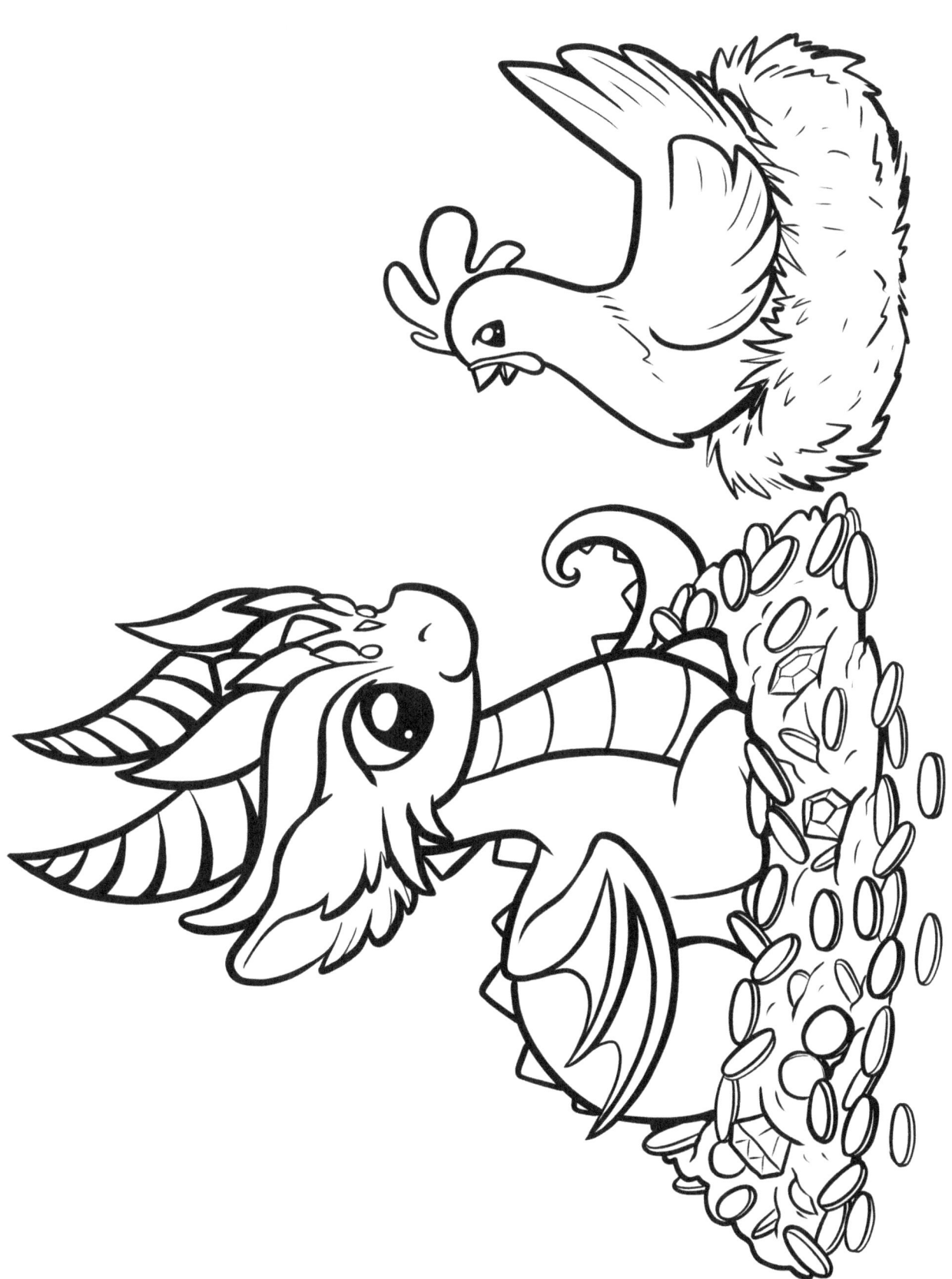

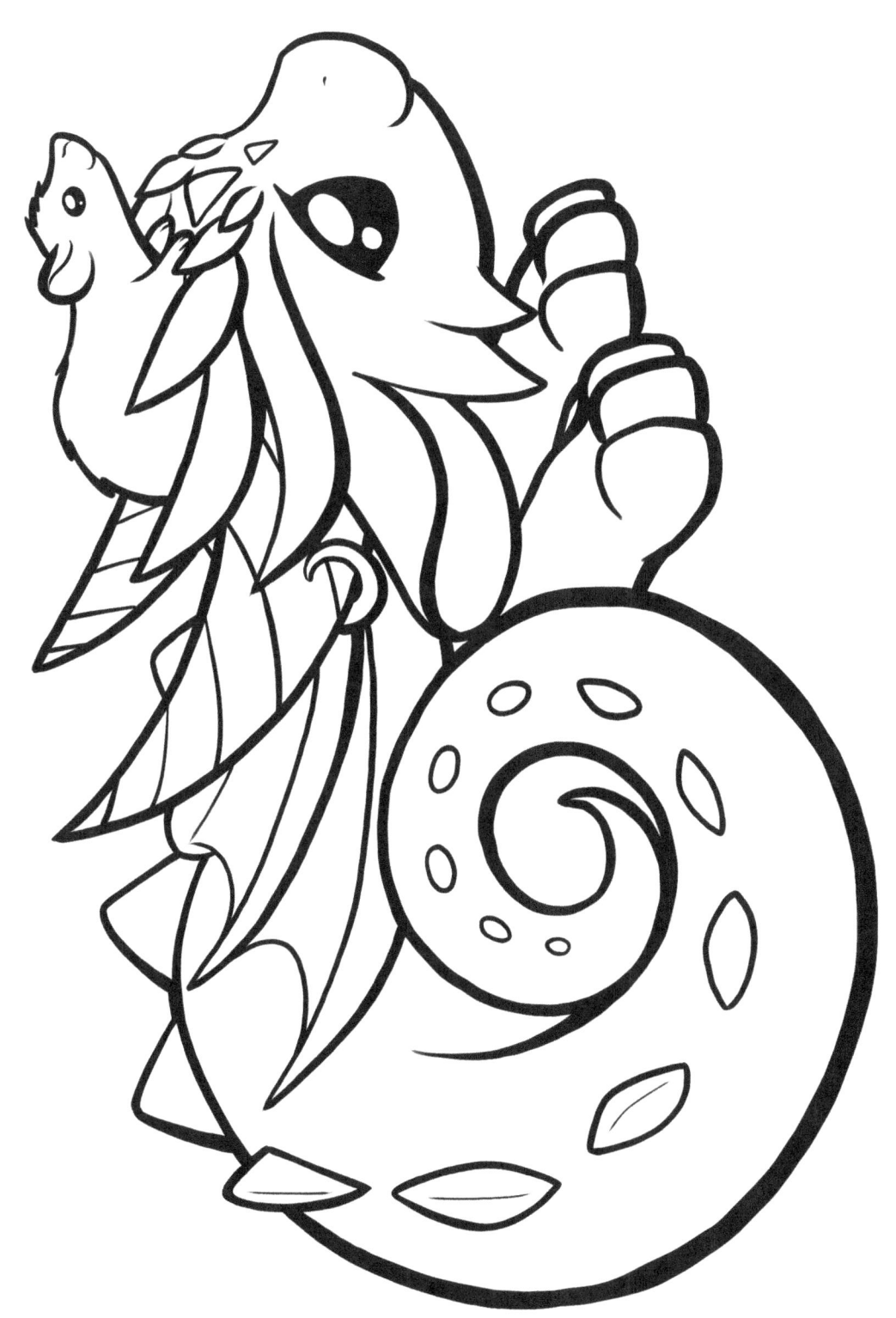

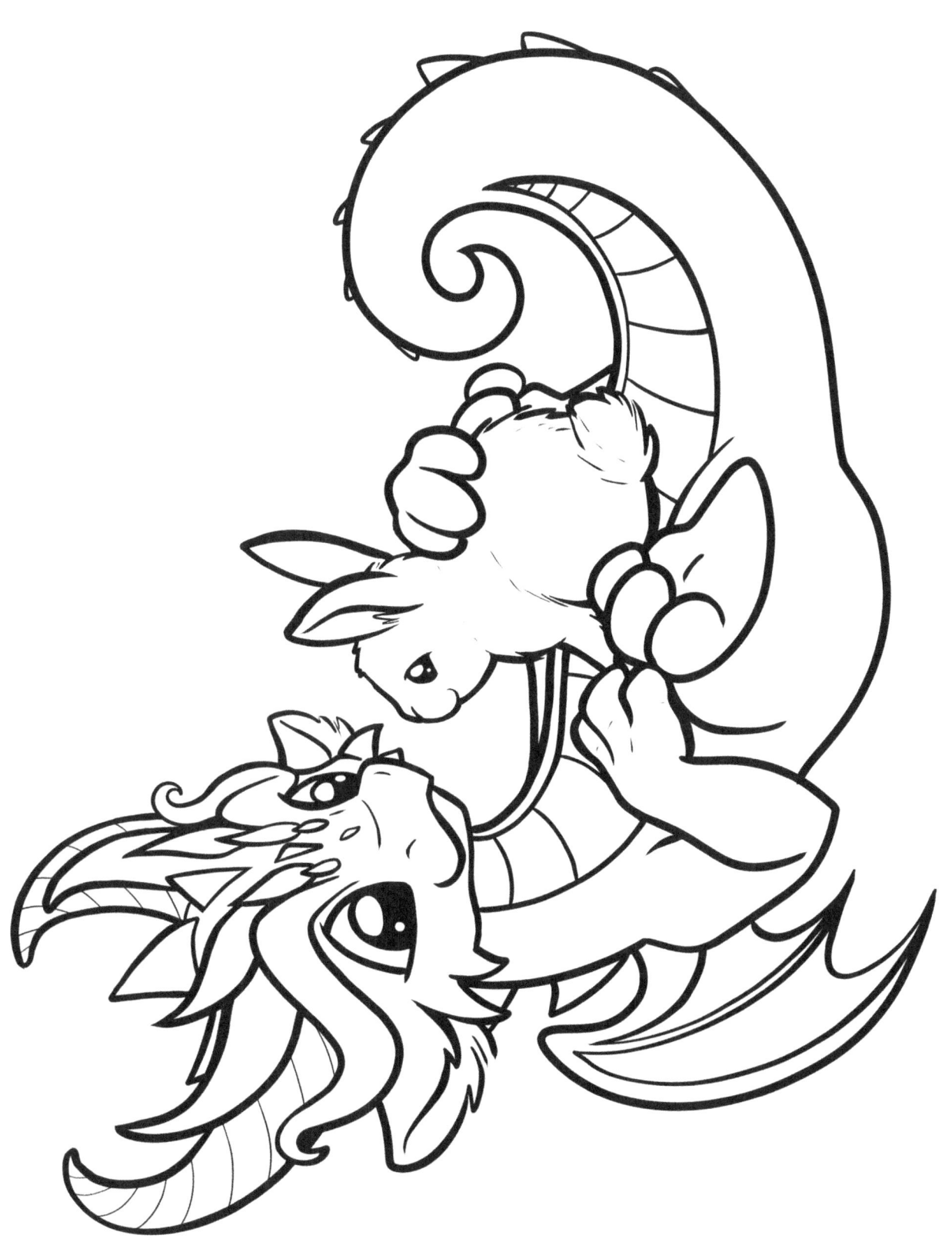

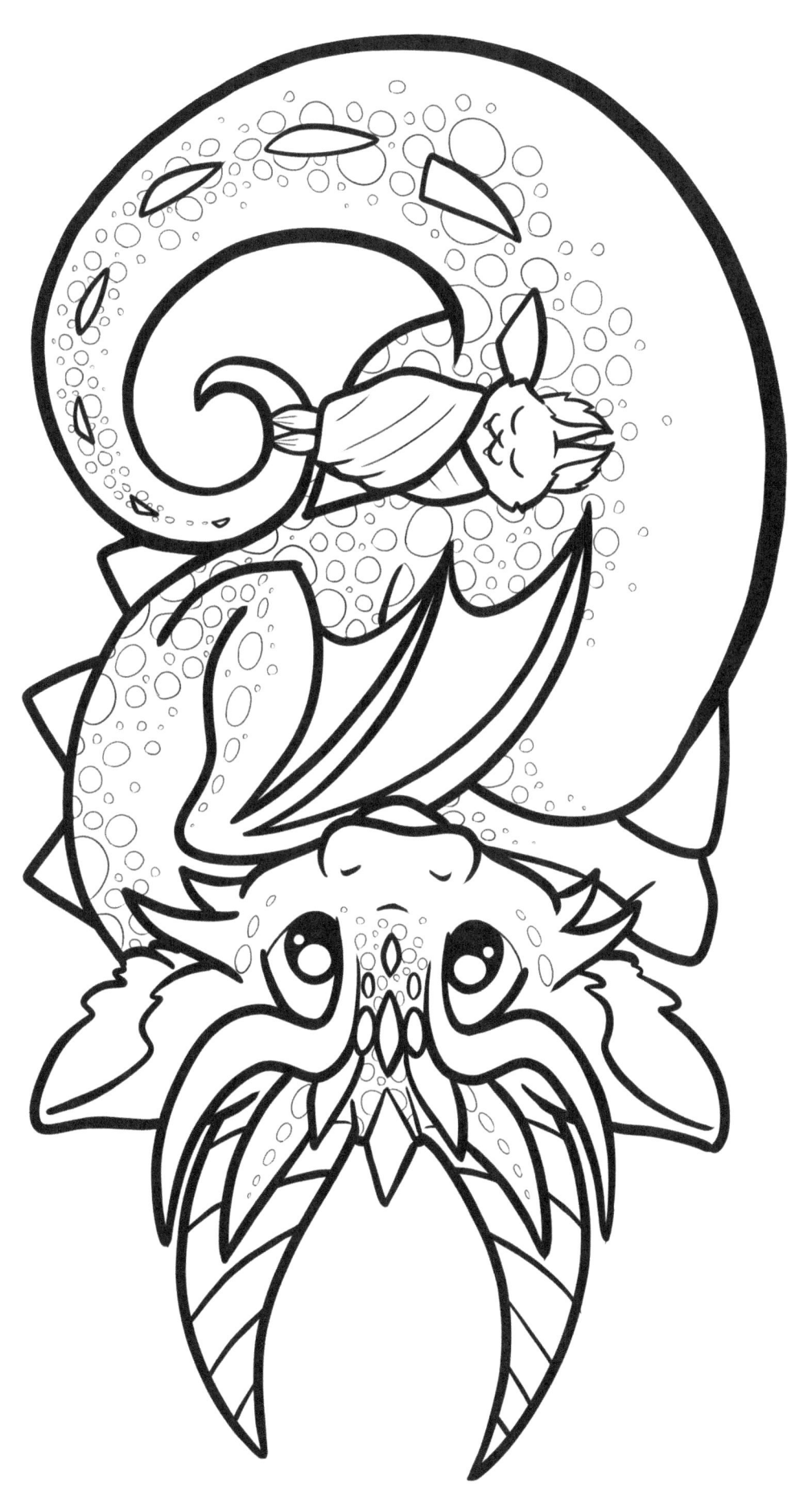

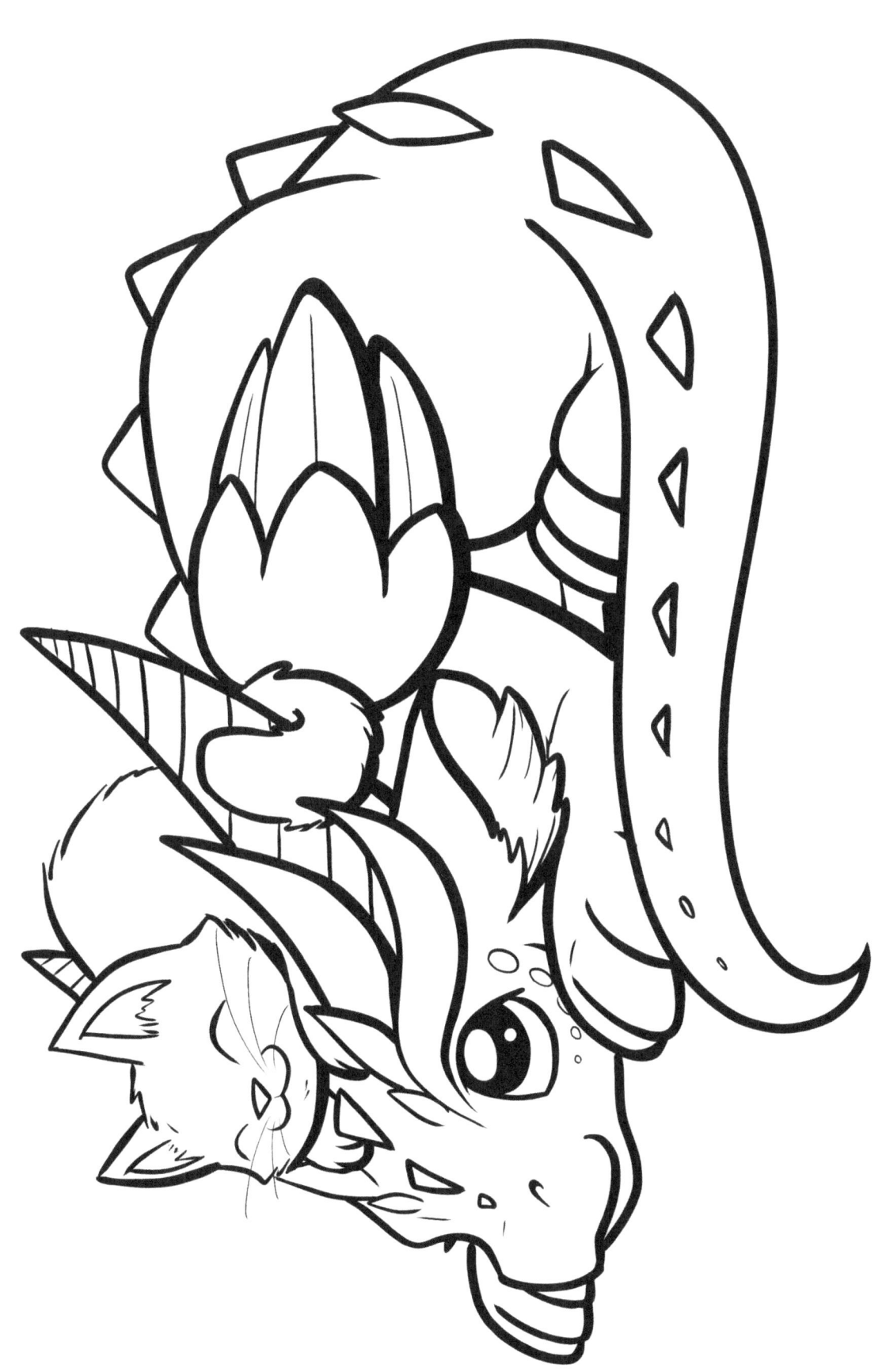